Monitor

Monitor

The Last Great Radio Show

Dennis Hart

Writers Club Press
San Jose New York Lincoln Shanghai

Monitor
The Last Great Radio Show

All Rights Reserved © 2002 by Dennis Hart

Writers Club Press
an imprint of iUniverse, Inc.

For information address:
iUniverse, Inc.
5220 S. 16th St., Suite 200
Lincoln, NE 68512
www.iuniverse.com

ISBN: 0-595-21395-2

Printed in the United States of America

To the men and women who made Monitor

Foreword

This book took about 40 years to write—and if that seems a tad too long, let me hasten to explain.

I was about 12 years old when, one Saturday in the living room in my California home, I was twisting the dial on my parents' big Grunow All-Wave Radio, looking for my favorite rock-radio station.

What I heard was, well, life-changing. Some strange, off-the-wall sound coming from that giant radio compelled me to stay tuned to a program I'd never encountered before—a show that sounded Very Big Time. For one thing, a guy I knew as "Mr. Magoo" was hosting it—Jim Backus. What in the world was *he* doing on the radio?

He was hosting *Monitor,* of course. And the sound that beckoned me was, of course, The Beacon—the *Monitor* Beacon. It introduced me to a whole new world of radio—to big-time hosts introducing big-name guests and going to a whole lot of different places all over the world. And all of this came from something called "Radio Central"—which sounded to my very young ears like the largest, most important radio place in the entire world.

Actually, it was.

I started living a "double life." During the week, I'd take my transistor radio (with its tiny ear plug) to school and pretend I was actually listening when my teachers lectured about sentence structure and about Washington's winter at Valley Forge and about all those math equations. Of course, my ear (the left one) was really hearing the Beatles, the Stones and even Peter and Gordon.

But on weekends, I forgot all about rock radio—I was fixated on *Monitor.* I began listening so much that I would plan my Saturday and

Sunday activities around the show. I didn't want to miss a second of Gene Rayburn and David Wayne and Ed McMahon and Barry Nelson and Frank Blair and Frank McGee and Henry Morgan and all the other big-name personalities who transported me to worlds I'd never even thought of.

I loved *Monitor*. And I even dragged a few of my friends into a serious relationship with the program.

Not, of course, as serious as mine—no way. In college, I majored in broadcasting because I wanted to work on *Monitor*. And when, to my great dismay, NBC canceled the program before I could "get there" (for some unfathomable reason, they just wouldn't hire this newly minted college grad)—I did the only thing I could.

I wrote a masters thesis about it.

That's how I got to meet Pat Weaver, who, simply, was the most creative genius in American broadcast history. He had created *Monitor* for his NBC Radio Network—and he was happy to talk about it with me, for several hours, in his Santa Barbara home. (No, his daughter Sigourney was not there at the time.)

By 1978, the thesis was done, but my interest in *Monitor* wasn't. Over the years, as I pursued a career in broadcasting and university teaching, I never lost interest in Mr. Weaver's creation. I continued researching the program—to the point where I had loads of material about *Monitor*, with no place to use it.

Then along came this new thing called the Internet—and a 16-year old son who could care less about radio but who spends every waking moment on the World Wide Web. I had the *Monitor* material, he had ability to magically put it "up there"—and the *Monitor* Tribute Pages were born in October 2000 (at http://www.monitorbeacon.com).

Yes, I was surprised no one had done it before.

In my wildest dreams, I never thought we'd receive more than a couple of hundred "hits" on the site in its first year. I missed the mark by nearly 10,000.

Apparently, there are lots of "you" out there who are just like me—you grew up (or grew older) listening to *Monitor* and somehow, in ways that I don't try to understand, you found the Tribute Pages. You began sharing your stories with me—and some of you urged me to write a book.

Again, I was surprised that no one had done it yet.

So now, 40 years after the Beacon and Jim Backus lured me to *Monitor* —you are holding a work that I trust will give you as much pleasure to read as it has given me to put together.

This book can by no means claim to be the "total" source of information about *Monitor,* but it is, I think, the best collection of information and anecdotes yet compiled about that wonderful show. And rest assured that this work is not designed to make me any money–indeed, any author proceeds will go toward establishing a journalism scholarship at my alma mater.

I hope you enjoy it, and that it brings back some great memories of our times on the *Monitor* Beacon.

And one more note–should you want to hear some of the sounds of *Monitor,* or see what Radio Central looked like, or look at some of *Monitor's* communicators over the years, check out the website at www.monitorbeacon.com. You won't be disappointed.

Acknowledgments

I have many to whom I am in great debt for their efforts on behalf of this book. They include several who had direct ties to *Monitor* and who generously offered their time for interviews: Pat Weaver, Melissa Blanton, Hugh Downs, Bud Drake, Charles Garment, Monty Hall, Jim Lowe, Bob Maurer, Tedi "Miss Monitor" Thurman, Steve White and Bob Wogan. In addition to speaking with me, Mr. White gave me a wonderful Christmas present years ago—a considerable amount of archival matter from NBC Radio, including tapes and print material.

And there have been many others who have contributed greatly to this project, including Jack Burns, Gary Dibble, Bob Dreier, the Rev. Douglas Drown, Thomas Frieling, Gene Garnes Sr., Gene Garnes Jr., Ralph Gould, Kenneth Johannessen, Earl Jones, Peter King, Don Kennedy, W.T. Koltek, Terry Morgan, Matt Ottinger, Joe Pugliesi, Ken Smith, Don Spuhler, Jim Willard and Bradley Hart.

And then there's Jim Wilson. Once the program director of an NBC Radio affiliate, now a university professor, Jim has urged me for more years than I care to remember to write this book. Once I did, he made valuable suggestions about how to make it better.

Thank you, Jim.

I appreciate everyone who has helped make this book a reality, and in the process, helped preserve a really important part of broadcast history.

Introduction

It became the greatest show in network radio history, the forerunner of talk radio and one of the most-copied formats ever. Its creator, the brilliant NBC President Sylvester L. "Pat" Weaver Jr., described it as a "kaleidoscopic phantasmagoria." Critics called it "Weaver's Folly."

To the rest of us, it was simply, and wonderfully, *Monitor*.

It was a program born out of inspiration and desperation. When *Monitor* made its splashy NBC Radio debut on Sunday, June 12, 1955, traditional network radio, with its half-hour and hour comedy, drama and variety shows, was in desperate shape. Television was stealing—had stolen—most of network radio's audience. In city after city, the arrival of TV resulted in drastic declines in the audience for the national radio shows.

In addition, many local radio stations were finding increased success with disk jockeys who played lots of music and mixed it up with frequent time and temperature checks—success that came at the expense of the formerly dominant radio networks.

It was clear that network radio needed something new and different—fast. And if anyone could deliver that, it was Weaver. Already in his brief NBC career, he had created the *Today, Tonight* and *Home* shows on his TV network—as well as the concept of "spectaculars," those 90-minute presentations that pre-empted regularly scheduled shows with big-name stars performing in showcased productions.

So Weaver went to work and came up with a format so audacious and grandiose that nothing like it had ever been heard on radio.

He called it *Monitor*.

On that premiere Sunday in 1955, *Monitor* aired on NBC Radio from 4 p.m. to midnight Eastern Time, with the first hour broadcast simultaneously on NBC-TV. Starting the following weekend, the program ran continuously for 40 hours, from 8 a.m. Saturday to midnight Sunday. It had everything—news, sports, comedy, interviews, remote pick-ups from around the world, music—a true magazine of the air.

It became a smash hit.

The lure of *Monitor* was that listeners could tune in or out at any time during the weekend wherever they were—in their homes, cars or on the beach—and not feel they had "missed" something. During any *Monitor* hour, dozens of different people, places and things were presented—all presided over, live, by hosts Weaver called "communicators" broadcasting from mammoth New York studios that NBC named "Radio Central."

Over the years, *Monitor* hosts included some of broadcasting's best and brightest stars—Dave Garroway, Frank Blair, Hugh Downs, David Brinkley, Gene Rayburn, Bert Parks, Mel Allen, Hal March, Frank McGee, Monty Hall, James Daly, Jim Backus, David Wayne, Ed McMahon, Barry Nelson, Henry Morgan, Jim Lowe, Joe Garagiola, Garry Moore, Durward Kirby, Murray the K, Bill Cullen, Cindy Adams, Art Fleming, Don Imus, Wolfman Jack, Robert W. Morgan and many, many more.

Classic comedians showed up on *Monitor* every weekend, including Bob and Ray, Nichols and May, Bob Hope, Jonathan Winters, Phyllis Diller, Ernie Kovacs, Bob Newhart and Woody Allen.

There was the inimitable "Miss Monitor," who made the weather sound like an "irresistible invitation to an unforgettable evening," as one critic gushed. At one time or another, every major TV, radio or movie star turned up at Radio Central for interviews. In addition, dozens of celebrity features and special reports brightened up each *Monitor* weekend, anchored by the likes of Arlene Francis, Curt Gowdy, Sandy Koufax, Gene Shalit, Dr. Joyce Brothers, The Galloping Gourmet and numerous others.

And, from the very first, there was The Beacon—the *Monitor* Beacon— a sound so unique that even today, decades after the show's demise, *Monitor* listeners can vividly recall how it signaled the start of the program or a cut-away for local station commercials.

Each weekend, *Monitor* promised listeners they'd be "going places and doing things," and then made it happen. During any "*Monitor* weekend," listeners could be transported to the world's biggest cities or smallest towns to meet some of the most important people around—or some of the quirkiest. Some of the sounds of *Monitor* were literally out of this world, while others were, well, just plain wacky.

This is the story of the radio program that, as Frank Blair put it, started as an experiment but ended up being an institution. It is the story of the men and women of *Monitor* and how they made it network radio's most important program—one that would capture more than 30 million listeners each weekend in a country of 180 million.

It is the story of the radio program that had such a huge impact on pop culture that its theme song was made into an album cut and *Playboy* magazine—the arbiter of all things "hip" and "hot" in the late 1950s —used the show as the punch line of a full-page cartoon.

For more than a thousand weekends, *Monitor* tied the country together electronically and provided news, sports and entertainment for a generation of Americans. It provided the very best programming that American radio had to offer. In the process, *Monitor* became NBC Radio's biggest advertising success story and kept the radio network alive for two decades.

But none of that mattered to its listeners, who merely wanted to tune in each weekend, no matter where they were or what they were doing, and hear the "Beacon" herald something new or interesting or important or fun or outrageous.

In the pages that follow, you will find out what made so many Americans make *Monitor* a weekend habit—and you will perhaps wonder why radio today has nothing remotely like the show that swept the country in the mid-20th century.

This is the story of *Monitor*—the Last Great Radio Show.

Contents

1

Pat Weaver's Great Idea

Pat Weaver knew his NBC Radio Network was in trouble—deep trouble. It was, after all, no secret. All of network radio was terminally ill—the victim of a disease spreading its way through America at the rate of thousands of homes each month.

That disease was television. It was killing the audience for traditional network radio programs.

Since the establishment of NBC Radio on November 15, 1926, listeners had become used to—even dependent upon—regularly scheduled 15-minute, half-hour or hour-long programs that brought music, comedy, variety, mystery and adventure into their homes each day or night on a schedule they could remember and rely on.

During the Great Depression and in the years that followed, network radio had brought the nation's biggest stars into virtually everyone's home, free of charge. During any given week, entire families would gather around the radio in the living room to listen to the likes of Bob Hope, Jack Benny, Edgar Bergen and Charlie McCarthy, Fibber McGee and Molly and to programs like *The Shadow*, *The Green Hornet* and *The Lone Ranger*—performers and shows lifting listeners out of their daily lives and into a world of make-believe that soothed day-to-day worries of a country heading from depression to war.

Then, during World War II, network radio magnificently rose to the occasion to bring up-to-the-moment eyewitness accounts of the fighting in Europe, Asia, Africa and the Pacific. Newscasters such as Edward R. Murrow, William Shirer, H. V. Kaltenborn and Elmer Davis became trusted household names as millions of Americans relied on them for their accounts and analyses of the war's progression.

After the war, the great radio networks—NBC, CBS, ABC and Mutual—continued their patterns of traditional programming, and their audiences stayed with them. But by then, the threat of television loomed. Indeed, NBC, CBS and, to a lesser extent, ABC, were sowing the seeds of their own destruction in radio because profits from their audio operations were being used to fund their experiments in television. By 1948, significant blocks of programming were airing on the television networks.

Still radio networks endured, primarily because the Federal Communications Commission "froze" the licensing of new TV stations in 1948 in order to study technical standards and frequency allocations. When the freeze was lifted in April 1952, less than a third of American homes owned TV's, and half of all those sets were concentrated in New York, Los Angeles, Chicago, Philadelphia, Boston, Detroit, Cleveland, Pittsburgh, St. Louis and Baltimore. (1)

By contrast, 98 percent of American families owned radios, and ratings for network radio were still relatively high. In early May 1952, CBS Radio's *Lux Radio Theatre* was the top-ranked weeknight program, reaching 4,750,000 homes. Weekday programs were topped by the CBS soap opera *Our Gal Sunday*, which was heard in 3,038,000 homes. (2)

But at year's end came word that radio network advertising sales had dropped 10 percent from 1951's total, prompting *Business Week* magazine to predict a future economic crisis for the networks and advance the theory that the nets would have to cut back on radio programming in order to reduce their losses. (3)

By the start of 1953, television penetration had skyrocketed in the United States, from 33 percent the previous year to 44 percent. (4) With that increase came a corresponding decrease in the audience for network radio programs. In 1953, the average nighttime network radio program had 100,000 fewer homes listening than in the previous year, and the networks were getting desperate for some good news. The major ratings company, Nielsen, tried to provide it with an announcement that "soon" it would develop a system to accurately measure radio listening in cars.

In May 1953, David Sarnoff, chairman of the board of NBC's parent company, the Radio Corporation of America (RCA), put on a brave face when he said that radio listening was changing from a family activity to one in which individuals listened in the privacy of their own rooms. Sarnoff offered the hope that there was still a solid basis for a "vigorous national radio service that can exist with television." (5)

Later that year, Sarnoff responded to another report that radios, which once had primarily been located in living rooms, were now all over typical American homes—and, equally importantly, were prevalent in car radios.

> *Present rating systems do not even credit this vast new audience to radio. They measure listening as if it were still 1947. It ignores listening to 5 million sets in public places, millions of portable sets, and more than 26 million automobile sets. Ratings today, simply do not reflect the real audience. (6)*

But the news kept getting worse for the radio networks. By early 1954, 58 percent of American homes had television, and the top-rated nighttime network radio show had one million fewer homes than the top-ranked evening show just a year earlier. Network radio was still doing okay in the daytime, but the nighttime audience was being siphoned away by television. And for the first time ever, the average daytime radio network show reached more people than the average network program at night. (7)

In late 1954, a new survey showed that the number of car radios was equal to the number of radios in living rooms across America. Radio networks took this to mean that they still commanded a big, though unmeasured, audience. Indeed, the first Nielsen reports on radio listening in cars seemed to confirm that.

That report in early 1955 showed that, in particular, weekend listening to network radio programs skyrocketed as much as 28 percent when listening in cars was added to the total. (8) But that was about the only good news the networks had to work with. By early 1955, the top-rated nighttime network show was heard in a million fewer homes than in the previous year.

What had happened to network radio in the preceding three years, since the end of the TV freeze, was easy to see. As television came into more and more American cities, radio network audiences declined as listeners became viewers. Jack Benny was still on radio, but fewer and fewer listeners cared—they wanted to watch him on TV.

And how did the radio networks react to all this bad news during the period from 1952 to 1955? They panicked. Radio networks began drastically cutting the amount of money they charged advertisers to be part of their network programs. Time after time during those years, individual networks would deny that rate cuts were imminent, only to turn around and cut those rates soon after the denial. The more the network audience declined, the more the rates were cut. "Uneasiness carrying almost hysterical overtones surrounded the network radio rate situation last week, with reports of ready-to-go nighttime cuts ranging all the way up to 60% despite repeated denials," wrote one trade magazine. (9)

The radio rate cuts failed to have the desired effect of keeping advertisers on board. By mid-1953, network TV advertising revenues passed radio's for the first time ever. (10) In 1954, total radio network income plummeted 11 percent over the previous year's. (11)

The networks weren't just cutting their advertising rates—they were trying new ways to sell commercial time as well. Until the early 1950s, the mainstay of network radio had been the binge advertiser who bought a full quarter-hour, half-hour or hour program. Now, the nets began going after smaller advertisers who might be able to buy only one commercial during a program. The networks called this type of purchase "spot" advertising.

Sarnoff recognized the need for radio nets to go after such "spots." "The economic basis for network radio was built on major advertisers and time-and-talent units of about a million dollars a year. It is for investments of that magnitude that television competes directly and successfully." (12)

Shortly after Sarnoff's comments, Pat Weaver took the helm of NBC as president. One newspaper critic offered the opinion that "life at NBC shouldn't be dull with Mr. Weaver in command." (13) Weaver, whose most recent job had been vice president in charge of NBC-TV, had an extensive background as a network radio producer, advertising agency pitchman and executive with a major tobacco company.

Almost immediately, Weaver announced plans to start new selling and program patterns for both his radio and TV networks to make sales to advertisers much easier. In early 1954, he put this philosophy to its first test by selling "spots" in a new Dave Garroway program on NBC Radio. Many of the network's affiliates objected to the plan because the spot prices forced them to lower their own rates in order to compete.

Late that year, Sarnoff, who just the year before had been optimistic about the future of network radio, now sounded his most pessimistic note ever:

> *I don't say that radio networks must die because every effort is being made and will continue to be made to find new patterns, new selling arrangements, and new types of programs that may arrest the declining revenues. It may yet be possible to eke out a poor existence for radio networks, but I don't know. (14)*

Besides cutting rates and trying new advertising patterns, the radio networks attempted to create new forms of programming to meet the challenges brought by television.

CBS Radio was the least innovative during this period, primarily because CBS had more top-rated programs than any other network. In general, CBS stuck with its "same time, same station" formula, in which listeners could tune in at the same time each day or night and catch the same program they had become accustomed to listening to at that hour over the years.

Mutual Radio, which alone among the Big Four radio networks did not also have a television network, was always in the weakest economic position among the nets. The reason was that while Mutual had more total radio affiliates than NBC, CBS or ABC, most of them were located in small towns and rural areas that major advertisers did not want to reach.

In the early 1950s, television spread out across the country from the biggest cities first. That fact helped Mutual survive for a time, because so many of its affiliates were outside the big cities and thus did not suffer the audience erosion that programs on the other radio networks did.

But by 1955, even Mutual was suffering from TV's inroads and began changing its nighttime programming into a more sports-oriented schedule. Other changes, the network promised, were forthcoming.

ABC Radio, which began its independent existence in the mid-1940s (15), had started tinkering with its programming as early as 1953, when it started producing nighttime shows on a "theme" basis. For example, on Saturdays, Sundays and Mondays, music predominated. Tuesday nights were devoted to lectures, while Wednesdays were designated as "Nights of Love." (16)

When that failed, ABC decided to cut its losses by becoming the first nighttime "music and news" radio network—essentially copying the formats of many local stations that had found success with disk jockeys who played lots of music interspersed with frequent "time and temperature" announcements.

NBC Radio made the boldest moves during the period from 1952 to 1955. Faced with CBS Radio's dominance as well as declining network ratings, NBC decided to try anything that might have a chance of working. In mid-1953, the network announced the premiere of 28 new programs for the fall radio season. A network vice president promised to "overwhelm the public with such a collection of new programs that they won't dare tune anyplace else for fear of missing something new and wonderful." (17)

Among the new programs: A Sunday afternoon "newspaper of the air" show from 4 to 6 p.m. Eastern Time called *Weekend* that would feature prominent radio personalities of the day such as Jinx Falkenberg, Earl Godwin, Leon Pearson and Mel Allen. The program interspersed remote reports from around the nation with music, sports, a women's page and new ideas in living.

At the same time, the network moved toward establishing "theme nights," with Mondays, for example, being devoted to music, Tuesdays to mystery and Wednesdays to comedy.

In January 1954, NBC Radio introduced a four-hour Saturday afternoon program called *Road Show*, which was designed specifically for drivers and included features such as safety driver awards and contests based on license plate numbers.

Virtually nothing worked. Radio network income continued to plummet to what one magazine called "catastrophic" depths. (18) The nighttime audiences had continued to wither, but daytime was holding steady. While network income levels were highly kept secrets, it was widely assumed that all four major radio networks were losing money. Experts were predicting that at least two of the four would fold by 1957—but they wouldn't, or couldn't, say which two. (19)

These were the dismal facts that Sylvester L. "Pat" Weaver Jr. faced. Arguably the most creative genius in the history of American radio and television, Weaver was already a media darling, and deservedly so. A national magazine once said of him that when it came to broadcasting, Weaver's dreams "are generally conceded to be the biggest and the best around," and that they had a "disconcerting habit of coming true." (20)

Weaver was born in Los Angeles in 1908, was graduated from Dartmouth College and went to work for Don Lee's regional radio network on the West Coast. He worked for a San Francisco radio station, then got a job with the mighty Young and Rubicam ad agency where, among other things, he produced the legendary Fred Allen's *Town Hall Tonight* network radio show.

At the tender age of 30, Weaver became advertising manager at George Washington Hill's American Tobacco Company. In 1949, he went to work for NBC as head of TV programming and then became President of the network.

To say that Pat Weaver revolutionized TV and radio would be a vast understatement. In the span of a few short years in the 1950's, Weaver created, among other things, *The Today Show, The Tonight Show, Home, Wide, Wide World* and the whole concept of "spectaculars" for his TV network. At the same time, he wrestled control of programming away from sponsors and created the idea of "magazine-style" advertising—instead of one sponsor owning or controlling the entire broadcast (the pattern under which network radio and television had been established), a series of "participating" advertisers would appear within the body of each program.

Weaver became known as broadcasting's most daring, most creative and most flamboyant executive. Everything he did, everything he created, was accompanied by a super-charged atmosphere of publicity. He loved the spotlight; he loved the adulation that came with his successes; and he loved what he did.

He was also extraordinarily good at his job.

Now Weaver turned his creative thoughts to the desperate state of NBC Radio, which had been bleeding red ink at least since 1952. The first official hint that he—and NBC—were up to something big came in *Broadcasting-Telecasting* magazine in February 1955. During the course of a long interview, Weaver revealed that NBC was working on a number of new things in radio, "one of them that we've had a lot of trouble in trying to work out, which I think will be announceable in '55." (21) Weaver went on to say the plan would give the network a five or ten-year view of radio as a business that was improving, and he called the plan "revolutionary."

That same month, *Variety* reported that NBC Radio was considering "tossing off the present Saturday-Sunday program schedules and installing a 48-hour weekend show to attract sponsors on a participating basis." The magazine said the program would in some ways be an extension of the network's current *Weekend* show on Sunday afternoons. (22)

Years later, Weaver revealed details of what had taken place. He explained that he had put together a group of people to work on the project that would lead to *Monitor*. One of the ideas discussed at the group's on-going meetings was to produce a radio network program similar to one which was then airing on WRCA Radio, NBC's New York station. There, station manager Steve White had instituted a program in response to a challenge from NBC's vice president in charge of owned-and-operated stations, Charles Denny:

> *Denny originally had asked for a contest for weekend programming between the program managers of the owned radio stations. The ground rules for the contest were to come up with something that was different, that you weren't doing before, that would result in increased sales. (23)*

White created a program on WRCA called *Pulse,* which aired on Saturday mornings from 10 until 11:30 a.m. He had an anchor, John Wingate, and several contributing reporters such as Lindsey Nelson on sports and Gabe Pressman on news. The program would showcase events of the upcoming day or weekend and review events of the past week.

Denny liked the idea and presented it to Weaver, who immediately thought it was something that could work for the network. In the biggest decision he would ever make involving radio—the one that would have the greatest ramifications not just for NBC but for the radio industry itself—Weaver "green-lighted" the creation of *Monitor.*

What Weaver knew was that old-time network radio was finished. No longer would audiences sit down for a radio program—they had to be "caught" wherever they were, at whatever they were doing. Weaver wanted a program that could be "taken with" listeners—travel with them to the beach, in their cars, on their vacations. He wanted a show that people could tune into at any time during the hour, without fearing they had "missed" something.

So, to his way of thinking, the new program had to have a wide variety of ever-changing elements in it—nuggets of information or entertainment long enough to grab the audience's interest but short enough not to bore them. In short, the program had to emphasize radio's increasing strength as a portable medium—something TV was not:

> *The* Monitor *concept…came from my conviction that if television had been invented first, by the nature of the need for people to be where they could watch the set pretty much to enjoy…that the medium of sound, radio only, audio only, would still have been developed as a national service. (24)*

After months of fine-tuning and the creation of prototypes, Weaver went public with the idea of *Monitor*. On Thursday, March 31, 1955, he and other NBC officials briefed members of the NBC Radio Affiliates Executive Committee and the Affiliates Study Committee. They asked NBC to explain the *Monitor* plan in a closed-circuit address to all NBC Radio stations the next day.

Weaver and Jim Fleming—who would become *Monitor's* first executive producer—went on the closed-circuit line to affiliates the next day—Friday, April 1. Weaver described the program as "a service tailored for you that will be highly interesting and amusing when you want it," and continued:

> *Essentially, we can once again have the whole American public know that any time in the weekend they need not be alone and they don't have to sit there looking at the television set—they can turn this service on and in will come the flow. It will be like having a personal editor who would go out and listen to everything, read everything, know everything, and then be there as your little cap and bells jester with the whole range of moods telling you the very best of everything that's happening. (25)*

Weaver told affiliates the program would have "more people on it and more important people saying things of high interest and repeatable values than probably anything that has ever been attempted." He described it as an around-the-clock weekend service that would go practically anywhere and do practically anything—a program that would break way from the traditional programming patterns of radio networks:

> *This is a rewrite of the (radio) medium as though it had never been before to do the greatest job and to be harnessed in the right way to do the greatest product selling job for our advertisers. And if it works right, we'll have the big audiences again although in a little different form. (26)*

Weaver told affiliates that he hoped *Monitor* would gain a 50 percent cumulative audience over the course of the weekend—that is, half of the American people would tune in sometime during the weekend. He outlined a sales plan that would encourage advertisers to buy "positions" scattered throughout the weekend in segments of one minute, 30 seconds and six seconds.

Fleming called *Monitor* an "entirely new sound and concept," a "complete departure from programming of the past." He played 15 minutes of recorded excerpts of what he described as possible segments of a *Monitor* program, including news from NBC reporter Morgan Beatty and analysis from newspaper columnist Art Buchwald; music from Paris; poetry from Ogden Nash; a horse race; a remote report from an airport where a jet plane was about to take off with a *Monitor* correspondent on board to report while it was in the air; audio highlights of comedian George Gobel "warming up" the audience for his TV show on NBC; and patter from Dave Garroway, who had become nationally famous as host of NBC's *Today Show.*

Fleming told affiliates that *Monitor* would use the full technical resources of NBC Radio to bring "a constantly changing pattern" of news, entertainment and music—"most of it live"—to listeners. The length of each segment would depend upon its importance and interest.

Weaver added that *Monitor* would be able to do many things and go to many places that television could not yet accommodate. He said that the program would get people talking about radio again.

Perhaps the most startling thing Weaver and Fleming told affiliates was that *Monitor* would toss aside the traditional clock pattern that network radio had developed and used for three decades. *Monitor* would begin every Saturday morning at 8 o'clock and run continuously until midnight Sunday—an unheard-of, almost incredible, 40-consecutive hours of broadcasting every weekend.

A few days later, NBC and Weaver held a press conference in New York to officially announce the creation of *Monitor*. Weaver told reporters the program would embrace everything from one-line jokes to 20-minute special remote pick-ups. A typical *Monitor* hour, he said, would include national news summaries on the hour, sports summaries, capsule entertainment attractions and features, and a five-minute cutaway on the half hour for news broadcasts by local stations in the network. In addition, *Monitor* would have live pick-ups of parts of NBC-TV programs and live or recorded vignettes from video rehearsals. Weaver also indicated that a group of famous personalities that he called "communicators" would be hired to preside over *Monitor*. (27)

During the press conference, Weaver created the colorful phrase that would be remembered forever to describe *Monitor*. He later explained that he thought it up on the spot:

> *We went through all of the vignettes and the personalities and the philosophy of extension and personal magnetism, all the different little pieces we were putting together in this little mosaic, and finally one of the chaps from the press got up and in what I considered to be a somewhat surly way and said, "Look, can't you just tell us what this program is in two*

words?" And I looked at him and I said, "Yes, it's a kaleido-scopic phantasmagoria," which of course broke up the group.
(28)

The phrase also apparently impressed the writers—the *New York Times* quoted it in the second paragraph of its next-day article about *Monitor*.

Weaver told reporters that *Monitor* would debut on Sunday, June 12, with its first hour "simulcast"—that is, broadcast simultaneously on NBC Radio and TV. This was a brilliant tactical move ensuring that anyone watching TV at that time—at least, anyone watching NBC-TV—would be shown not only that a new radio program was being introduced, but that radio actually still existed.

And it was a move that helped guarantee major press coverage of *Monitor* in the coming weeks. For what Weaver had done in his typical flamboyant style was to make *Monitor* sound like much more than a new radio program—there had been, after all, "new" radio programs since the beginning of the medium 35 years earlier. Weaver had made *Monitor* sound like the most exciting radio program ever.

Now he had to deliver.

2

Assembling the Cast

Dave Garroway didn't want anything to do with *Monitor*. He didn't even want to do an audition for the soon-to-debut program because he considered it a waste of time—almost certainly, he thought, *Monitor* was going to fail.

"It sounded too chopped up," he said. "Too shot-in-the-arm-y." (1)

But Pat Weaver—that master showman, the former advertising ace who knew how to sell almost anything—understood that *Monitor* needed—absolutely had to have—big-name TV people hosting the new weekend show in order to generate the type of excitement and tune-in that could make the program a success. Those big names were so important that Weaver wouldn't just call them "hosts"—he would designate them as "communicators," the same name he gave his *Today Show* hosts on TV.

And Dave Garroway was very nearly the biggest name—the biggest "communicator"—in television at the moment.

Garroway was born in Schenectady, New York, the son of a "troubleshooting" engineer who frequently had to move to new job sites. The family finally settled for a time in St. Louis, where Dave went to high school and Washington University. He majored in psychology and English. (2)

One night in New York, a friend invited him to a bridge party attended by a woman from the NBC personnel staff. She persuaded Garroway to apply for a job as an NBC page—a position that, for decades, proved to be the entry "key" for many people who aspired to network radio (and, later, TV) careers. Garroway got the job. It paid $16.65 a week. (3)

During his spare time, Garroway studied announcing, took a class in it and finished 23rd out of 24 students. That was good enough to get him a job offer from the legendary KDKA Radio in Pittsburgh—the first licensed radio station in the United States. There, he handled a variety of special events, including announcing from the backs of polo ponies, submarines and canoes.

Taking a vacation in Chicago, Garroway decided to audition for a job at WMAQ Radio—and got it. He became the station's general announcer in 1939.

Shortly after World War II began, Garroway joined the Navy and ran a yeoman school in Honolulu for most of the war. Again, his "spare time" led him to announcing, this time as a disk jockey on a local radio station. He played jazz and filled the show with "small talk"—and in the process developed the trademark communication style that would propel him to the top of the broadcasting field.

Back in Chicago and WMAQ after the war, Garroway got another radio job—as host of a midnight jazz and talk show. That led to his first TV job in 1948—a program called *Garroway at Large,* a network variety show that exploited his by-then fully developed "style" of casual, almost intimate conversation.

By 1951, Pat Weaver was deeply involved with remaking NBC-TV in his own image. He decided the time was ripe to "open up" the early morning hours on his network—to try to take away listeners from the nation's radio stations by essentially putting a radio show on TV. His vision was a two-hour program full of news, music, interviews, weather forecasts and helpful tips. He would call it *Today.*

Garroway found out about Weaver's plans about the time that *Garroway at Large* was canceled by the network. He set up a meeting with a *Today* producer in Chicago, then flew to New York for an audition. Two days later, he was named *Today's* first host—or "communicator," as Weaver insisted on naming him.

The program debuted on Jan. 14, 1952, and it quickly became clear that Garroway was, indeed, the perfect choice as host. His informal, unruffled style—his wide knowledge about an immense variety of subjects—and his uncanny ability to remain calm while everything was falling apart around him and the show—all worked together to create the perfect type of atmosphere for an early-morning TV program.

By 1955, Garroway was as well-known as any performer in television. So when Weaver decided, in essence, to re-create *Today* on weekends and call it *Monitor*, Garroway was the first name that came to his mind as host.

But the *Today* host wanted no part of *Monitor*, at least at first:

> *Pat Weaver's assistant came into the office, and I was lying down,*
> *I remember, and he said, "Dave, uh, we want you to do a show*
> *on radio. We're going to call it* Monitor, *and it's going to be…"*
> *Then he went into a kind of vague description, and I sat there,*
> *and I said, "No, Alan, I don't think it's gonna work, I'd rather*
> *not, if you don't mind."*
> *Then he came back a couple hours later and said, "Pat would like*
> *you to do it very much as a personal favor to him." And I said,*
> *"Well, if Pat wants me to do it, I'll do anything for Pat." (4)*

And so it was that Garroway was the first "name" that NBC revealed as a host, or communicator, of the upcoming *Monitor*.

The next communicators to be announced were Goodman and Jane Ace, two veterans of network comedy whose longtime show, *The Easy Aces*, was one of the earliest hits in radio. As good as they were, their entire radio careers might well have been considered an accident.

One night in the late 1920s, Goodman Ace, a newspaperman who had been hired by a Kansas City radio station to do movie reviews, was finishing his on-air duties when the program director motioned to stay on the air. As was common in those days, the "next act" had failed to show up.

So Goodman Ace began to ad-lib, and his wife Jane, who was standing nearby, joined in. They talked about events of the day, last night's card game—anything to fill time. The audience loved it.

That started them on the road toward network stardom. Their *Easy Aces* program essentially was a dialogue between the two—Goodman, who came across as witty and charming—and Jane, who came across as the mistress of misinformation. The result was often hilarious.

After their network radio run ended, Goodman Ace became a comedy writer for a number of network TV shows. On *Monitor,* they were expected to recreate some of the comedy magic that had worked for them for so long on radio. (5)

One of the next hosts to be announced was Walter Lanier Barber—known to almost every sports fan simply as "Red." By the time "Red" Barber became a *Monitor* host, he had already put in 25 years as one of the country's most famous sports announcers.

By 1955, Barber had covered 13 World Series, four All-Star baseball games, and five Army-Navy, Orange Bowl and Rose Bowl football classics. (6) He had been a radio voice of the Cincinnati Reds, Brooklyn Dodgers and New York Yankees. He was certainly one of the best-loved sports personalities of his era.

Clifton Fadiman was also persuaded to become a *Monitor* communicator. Fadiman had a long and distinguished career in print, as an editor and critic for *The New Yorker* magazine. But many American radio listeners knew him as the moderator of a long-running "intellectual" quiz show on radio called *Information Please.* There, he presided over a panel that included *New York Times* sports columnist John Kieran, newspaper columnist Franklin Pierce Adams and assorted personalities from the fields of entertainment and politics.

John Cameron Swayze was also signed for a stint on *Monitor.* Since 1948, Swayze had been host of NBC-TV's evening newscast. Originally called *The Camel Newsreel Theater,* the program began as a 10-minute production. A year later, it expanded to 15 minutes and was renamed the *Camel News Caravan.*

Swayze became known for the carnation he always put in his lapel and for the phrase he always used near the end of his program: "Now let's go hopscotching the world for headlines." (7) He brought 20 years of journalistic experience in newspapers, radio and TV to the anchor desk, and by 1955 was widely known as one of the nation's most important news personalities.

While Swayze handled NBC's signature evening newscast, Frank Blair was handling news on the *Today Show.* Blair—who had a long background in radio reporting—had appeared on the very first *Today* as its Washington correspondent. He so impressed network staffers that he was asked to move to New York to anchor the morning news segment of the broadcast.

It made sense, of course, for Blair to be on *Monitor*—after all, Garroway was going to be there, and Weaver loved the thought of having his TV people host this most important of all radio projects.

But while Blair wanted to do it, he had a special problem: His current contract with NBC forbade him from reading commercials. How could he possibly host a show that Weaver hoped would be a smash commercial success without being able to read the commercials that would make it so?

NBC fixed matters by hiring another voice—Don Russell—to co-host with Blair. Russell was an announcer whose contract did not prohibit him from reading commercials. Thus, Russell and Blair would become a "team" on *Monitor*—they were scheduled from 8 a.m. to noon on Saturdays—and they would have the distinction of being the first "communicators" heard when the program began its regular broadcast schedule, one week after the premiere. (8)

In 1955, Hugh Downs was known primarily as Arlene Francis' co-host on NBC-TV's *Home Show.* He had been a broadcaster since the late '30s and had worked at NBC in Chicago on both radio and TV. In 1954, Weaver dreamed up a midday TV show catering to housewives and their needs and desires. Well-known New York radio announcers Gene Rayburn and Ben Grauer and others were being considered for the co-hosting role opposite Arlene Francis:

> *And then they decided that all these people were so well-known locally already that it would be kind of old hat. So they decided to go with somebody new and import somebody. I came there to do what amounted to an audition. At the last minute, when they did the last rehearsal, before the next day's (debut), they had not made a decision. And I remember Pat Weaver standing in this specially constructed studio, and I came up to him and said, "Mr. Weaver, should I go back to Chicago and forget about it? Who are you going to use?" He thought a minute and said, "Oh, we'll go with you." I started the next day. (9)*

Home was divided into sections—beauty care, cooking, fashions and more. Ad-libbing was the order of the day, and that role fit Downs perfectly. He was low-key; he was quick-witted; audiences, particularly women, seemed to like him; and he seemed "natural" and at-ease on the air.

Weaver thought he would be a "natural" for *Monitor.* So Hugh Downs, just a year after arriving at the "big time" in New York TV, was signed to host the biggest radio show of his life. He would become the Saturday afternoon *Monitor* host, following Frank Blair's Saturday morning segment.

Morgan Beatty was a longtime NBC Radio newsman in 1955. He had been a distinguished World War II correspondent, had anchored the radio network's nightly *News of the World* for years and had briefly anchored a newscast on the DuMont television network in the early 1950s. He became a *Monitor* contributor, sometimes co-hosting the show and other times reading the news.

Walter Kiernan was a newspaperman who had become a familiar face on early-day TV. He hosted a variety of game and interview programs for various TV networks, including *Greatest Moments in Sports, Kiernan's*

Corner, That Reminds Me, What's the Story? and *Who's the Boss?* For NBC, he had spent four years hosting *Who Said That?* on both radio and TV. He also joined the growing list of *Monitor* communicators.

Henry Morgan did not become one of the original *Monitor* hosts. Instead, he was signed to become *Monitor's* "TV monitor." NBC said that each weekend night, Morgan would show up and "will monitor television for *Monitor* and report his observations to radio listeners." (10) That those observations would be witty, acerbic and probably outrageous was a given.

Morgan was known as radio's original "bad boy"—and for good reason. Starting with his on-air radio debut in the early 1930s, and through a succession of announcing jobs in Philadelphia, Duluth, New York and Boston, Morgan did something that advertisers hated: He joked about, and sometimes made fun of, their products.

In 1940, when he turned up at WOR Radio in New York, Morgan took his "kidding" to new heights. On his nightly 15-minute *Here's Morgan* show on WOR and Mutual Radio, Morgan occasionally lambasted his sponsors, to the point where some of them pulled their commercials from his show. If his radio bosses criticized him for losing advertising, he would castigate them on the air for doing so. Morgan became known as a loose cannon—and as a quick wit who could ad-lib for long periods of time and "carry" a program by himself, if the need arose. (11)

Morgan became one of the first radio performers to jump into television. In 1948, he briefly hosted ABC-TV's first network series—a program called *On the Corner,* in which he would read the pages of *Variety* magazine to reveal the names of his guests. He also did what he had become known best for on radio—tossed in critical remarks about his sponsor, the Admiral Corporation. The program lasted five weeks. (12)

He often showed up on early TV game shows as a panel member. One of those appearances cemented his name as a bona fide television star. Five months after the debut of a CBS-TV program called *I've Got a Secret,*

Morgan became a regular on the panel. He would remain there until the end of the program's original network run in 1967.

Morgan and *Monitor* would be linked off and on for much of the radio program's life. He would return again and again, as a contributor and as a host. He often would introduce himself with the phrase, "Here's Morgan," referring, for those with good memories, to the title of his nightly network program 15 years earlier.

There was no question that *Monitor* was making news just by signing such big-name personalities. But Weaver knew that something more was needed to put the program "over the top"—to generate the kind of tune-in, and repeat listening, that would make it work. He needed a gimmick.

Years earlier, Weaver's *Today* on NBC-TV had floundered with both audiences and advertisers until a chimpanzee named J. Fred Muggs came on board and saved the day. Muggs provided the unpredictable comedy relief that attracted audiences and guaranteed that people would be talking about *Today* when they got to work or saw their friends.

But Muggs was a visual act, so there would be no thoughts of chimps on *Monitor*. But there would be a gimmick—in fact, two of them—each so good, so outrageous, so "out there" that, to this day, *Monitor* listeners of that time can still recall them vividly.

Bob Elliott and Ray Goulding made comedy magic almost by accident. In 1946, they were both working at a Boston radio station—Bob as a morning disk jockey and Ray as his newscaster. They began ad-libbing on-air remarks after Ray's newscasts—and listeners took notice.

They created characters such as Wally Ballou, Mary McGoon and Charles the Poet. They did parodies of then-favorite radio soap operas, changing the name of *One Man's Family* to "One Feller's Family." They expanded their comedy universe to include such routines as "Jack Headstrong, the All-American American," (a takeoff on the popular network series *Jack Armstrong, the All-American Boy*) and "Mr. Trace, Keener Than Most Persons" (a parody of *Mr. Keen, Tracer of Lost Persons*).

Their careers skyrocketed. In 1951, NBC hired them to do a 15-minute evening show on the radio network. That show turned into a half-hour Saturday night radio program. Then they went on a local station in New York opposite the dominant morning team of Gene Rayburn and Dee Finch—and almost immediately began taking ratings away from the other duo.

They did a TV series for ABC, then returned to local radio in 1954. (13)

Hiring Bob and Ray to appear on *Monitor* was not just a brilliant move—it was inspired.

Because what they were told to do was not just to perform a comedy routine now and then. They were brought on board to stay at Radio Central the entire weekend—all 40 hours—and be ready to ad-lib a comedy routine whenever something "went wrong"—that is, whenever a remote report failed to turn up, or a telephone line went down during a correspondent's report or a tape broke during playback of a feature.

They were hired as "back-ups"—and they would, as it turned out, perform that role so well, so memorably, that their place in comedy history would be cemented by their many appearances on *Monitor*.

Bob and Ray were two of the keys that made *Monitor* an almost instant hit. The other was Weaver's second "gimmick."

Her real name was Tedi Thurman. She was a fashion model with a few TV credits who had been noticed by an NBC staffer who thought she might be good on Pat Weaver's upcoming radio show.

On *Monitor*, Tedi Thurman lost her identity. She became known as "Miss Monitor," and what she did had never been done in quite the same way before on radio.

"Miss Monitor" delivered weather forecasts in a way that was, to say the least, unusual. She read the forecasts in a sexy, sultry voice with lush, romantic music playing in the background.

And that was all she had to do to become a smash hit. For the rest of her life, Tedi Thurman would be known as "Miss Monitor." Long after she left *Monitor*, she would be asked to perform her weather routine wherever she went.

"Miss Monitor" and Bob and Ray were the icing on the cake for Weaver to propel the program into listeners' consciousness.

Of course, the program's 40-hour marathon schedule required the hiring (or reassigning from other NBC programs) of dozens of other people—hosts, producers, directors, writers, editors, technical directors. All of them played key roles in putting *Monitor* on the air and keeping it there for an entire weekend, every weekend of every year for nearly two decades.

Among those early staff members were producers Arnold Peyser, Allen Ludden (who would go on to TV stardom as host of *Password*), Herb Hirschman, Fred Weihe, Marx Loeb and Ev Lifschultz, along with writers Tom Koch, Gordon Fraser, Jerry Smith, Murray Burnett and Bill Bales. Mike Zeamer became Saturday supervisor as well as a program writer. Al Capstaff was brought on board as a co-communicator and talent supervisor (he would later become the program's executive producer), Frank Papp was named Sunday supervisor and Burroughs (Buck) Prince supervised news and special events, working with Capi Petrash. Several production assistants were also hired.

Before this hiring "frenzy," one of Weaver's most important decisions was whom to bring on board as the "glue," the person in charge of making sure that somehow, this "kaleidoscopic phantasmagoria" got on the air each weekend.

He chose James Fleming, a veteran newsman, as the first executive producer of *Monitor*. Fleming and Weaver had worked together before—Fleming had been the first newscaster on the *Today Show*.

Now Weaver gave him the reins of *Monitor*. Fleming's job was to pull together all of the resources of the NBC Radio Network—the electronics and the people—and mesh them into a program that would be exciting, entertaining, and a "must-listening" experience for the audience.

It was no exaggeration to say that the future of NBC Radio depended on how well Fleming and Weaver succeeded.

3

Radio Central and The Beacon

Perhaps the first time the phrase "Radio Central" was heard outside NBC's corporate headquarters at 30 Rockefeller Plaza in New York was on Friday, April 1, 1955. Jim Fleming, who had been named *Monitor's* first executive producer, used the term in the closed-circuit message he and Pat Weaver made to radio network affiliates to announce the new *Monitor* service:

> *A few moments ago I walked by what used to be the NBC master control room on the fifth floor of the RCA Building, and believe me, some changes are being made. Workmen are beginning the construction of* Monitor's *home base, NBC Radio Central, a communications center that will really be in touch with the world.*
> *I have the sketches here before me—an immense communicators' desk in the center. At the broadcaster's command, a battery of switches placing him instantly in touch with all the domestic and overseas pick-up points. Newsroom on one side, tape room on the other, auxiliary studios—it's going to be quite a place. (1)*

In a short period of time, "Radio Central" would become synonymous with *Monitor*—almost as much a part of the program as the hosts and

24

features. It would, indeed, become part of the *Monitor* mystique. Communicators and contributing reporters would repeat the term "*Monitor* in Radio Central" so often that many listeners would come to know exactly where *Monitor* originated—in Radio Central, of course.

That type of knowledge was practically unheard of for network radio programs. How many listeners knew, or cared, where Jack Benny, Burns and Allen or Edgar Bergen originated their programs? Yes, some shows had fictional locations that played prominent roles in their plots—for example, listeners knew that Fibber McGee and Molly lived at 79 Wistful Vista—but actual studio locations were not considered important enough to be promoted along with the program.

Until *Monitor,* that is. NBC made sure that everyone knew that *Monitor* was so special that it required a state-of-the-art studio that just may have been the world's best. So well was Radio Central known that reviewers commenting about *Monitor's* first broadcast would also take time to mention the studio.

The network began its publicity barrage about Radio Central with a press release on April 15, 1955. Calling it a "last word in broadcasting operation," NBC said that the new $150,000 facility represented the ultimate in broadcasting flexibility:

> *Here the communicators…literally will be in touch with the world. By merely pushing buttons, the communicator will be able to establish live two-way communication both overseas and in this country, or even a round-table discussion involving several correspondents anywhere in the world.*
>
> *The control console at which the communicator will be seated provides for 24 different sources of monitoring, both foreign and domestic. At his disposal are trans-Atlantic telephone and overseas broadcast circuits, special broadcast lines and long-distance telephone lines for communication within the United States. (2)*

Radio Central would, the press release stated, permit the handling of 12 individual pick-up points at one time. In addition, *Monitor's* communicator of the moment would be in contact with roving NBC correspondents operating Ford Thunderbird units positioned around the nation, ready to report whatever important news story they could get to.

Also, the communicator would have a television monitor in front of him, carrying whatever NBC-TV program happened to be on the air at the time.

> *By flicking a switch, the communicator can pick up the television audio, whether it be a George Gobel monologue or a song by Gordon MacRae. Thus, the television network provides* Monitor *listeners with an important source of entertainment and information. (3)*

There was more. The NBC newsroom was being moved to become "a vital adjunct to Radio Central." Items of extreme importance, called "flashes," could be brought to the communicator "in a matter of seconds." News writers would be on continuous duty.

Another room next to Radio Central would contain "the most modern tape-recording equipment in the world." In that room, foreign and domestic feeds would be taped, edited and readied for broadcast on *Monitor.*

Announce booths on either side of Radio Central were being built. NBC reported that there were 18 microphones between the newsroom, Radio Central and the announce booths. All in all, Radio Central was to become a virtual world listening post:

> *In the original planning of Radio Central, the best minds in the design group and those with practical operating experience held numerous discussions to evolve the concept of Radio Central. The physical result is the last word in a broadcasting operation solely designed to keep listeners in instantaneous touch with the world. (4)*

NBC's publicity about Radio Central paid off handsomely. In his review the day after *Monitor's* first broadcast, *New York Times* media critic Jack Gould noted that "the headquarters of the show is a new studio called 'Radio Central,' equipped with all the gadgetry necessary to make pick-up from everywhere." (5)

Variety also mentioned Radio Central, as did *Time* and *Newsweek* magazines. *Newsweek* described it as "a vast expanse of plate glass and in the midst of myriad dials, plugs, knobs, switches and pale apple green walls." (6)

Printers' Ink magazine went one step farther, publishing several pictures of the facility and talking about "the large crew of communicators in Radio Central." (7)

Pat Weaver and his publicists had done it. They had made Radio Central an integral part of the *Monitor* story. From the beginning of the show to its end 20 years later, the term "*Monitor* in Radio Central" would be a part of the program's aura.

In spite of that, there would be at least one person who didn't "get it." His difficulties in understanding the concept of "*Monitor* in Radio Central" proved to one of the funniest "outtakes" in the program's history.

He was the "stringer" (a correspondent who was not an NBC employee but filed reports independently to *Monitor)* who was sending in a ski report from the West Coast.

That report was being taped for later airing by *Monitor* sports producer Roy Silver:

REPORTER: It was a terrific race, and the weather was clear.
SILVER: Where's my close?
REPORTER: What?
SILVER: Where the hell is the close? Will you identify yourself and say, "And now back to *Monitor* at Radio Central"?
REPORTER: All right. Ready? I'll take five. This is (name) a ski reporter from San Francisco. I'd like to return you back to *Monitor* in San Francisco.

SILVER: Look, uh, kid, you say your name is (name)?
REPORTER: Yes.
SILVER: Would you please say, "This is (name) in Squaw Valley.
Now back to *Monitor* in Radio Central."
REPORTER: All right. (PAUSE) This is (name) from Squaw Valley.
Now back to Radio *Monitor.*
SILVER: Let's try it again. It's *Monitor* in Radio Central.
REPORTER: *Monitor* in Radio Central. All right. This is (name)
from Squaw Valley. And now back to Radio *Monitor* in Central.

(LAUGHTER FROM CONTROL ROOM)

SILVER: Kid, let's try it slow this time, huh?
REPORTER: Let me write it down.
SILVER: And it's *Monitor* in Radio Central.
REPORTER: *Monitor* in Radio Central. All right. This is (name)
from Squaw Valley. And now back to *Monitor* in Radio Central. (8)

Most of the time, correspondents and communicators had no such
trouble remembering "*Monitor* in Radio Central."

The studio's name—and the facility itself—had a way of impressing
people. Gene Garnes Jr.—whose father helped engineer *Monitor* for many
years—remembers visiting the giant "listening post of the world" as a
youngster:

> *You have to understand that as a small child, Studio 5B*
> *seemed as big as a warehouse to me. It was definitely the*
> *coolest radio studio in the (RCA) Building at the time. They*
> *had couches scattered about, flowers in vases, and sometimes,*
> *a grand piano would be in one corner complete with a boom*
> *stand with an RCA 77DX hanging from it.*
> *I was so impressed; here was a room, where Gene Rayburn, a*
> *TV show host, was announcing and people across the country*
> *were listening to it. But it just wasn't that alone. There were*

all these incoming feeds from all over the world coming into
Radio City and being fed out live to the whole country. Here
would be someone from Germany talking live to Gene
Rayburn! Or a live report from a Vietnam battlefield being
fed live to the net. (9)

Yes, Radio Central became an integral part of *Monitor*—and so did a certain sound associated with the program.

It was officially called the *Monitor* Beacon—and it was so distinctive that, to this day, virtually everyone who listened to *Monitor* remembers and can describe it.

It was not unusual for distinctive sounds or themes to come to identify network radio programs. For many years, a creaking door punctuated the terrifying open to radio's *Inner Sanctum Mysteries*. Dramatic sound effects were a staple of another horror series, *Lights Out*. And, of course, the sound of Fibber McGee getting buried under junk when he opened his closet door became one of network radio's longest-running gags.

But the *Monitor* Beacon would be used far more extensively than other radio themes or identifiers. It would remain the one constant in the program's 20-year life. Other show elements would change—hosts, contributors, music, formats—but the Beacon remained. It would, in fact, be among the last things *Monitor* listeners would hear 20 years after they first heard it.

The Beacon took an amazing amount of engineering expertise to produce:

NBC decided upon a sound that is a combination of high fre-
quency tones dialed by an operator to activate remote telephone
equipment in completing long-distance calls. This sound was
recorded by the phone company and sent to NBC, which re-
recorded the sound at higher and lower frequencies, put it
through various filters and mixed it with a micro-second lag.
NBC engineers then superimposed an oscillator sending the
Morse Code letter "M"—for Monitor. (10)

The Beacon was hard to make and impossible to forget. But listeners almost didn't get a chance to hear it because one man—one very important man—didn't like it. In fact, David Sarnoff, the chairman of the board of RCA (NBC's parent company), hated the Beacon.

Pat Weaver got into what he called "a big fight" with Sarnoff over that sound:

> *He didn't know anything. He thought it would irritate people because it irritated him. I said, "General, we don't care about, really, about what you think because, you know, we're really doing it for the population. I don't expect you to listen to the show." (11)*

Weaver won, and the Beacon became a key part of the program for its entire broadcast life. It would be used to "open" each segment of the broadcast. It became the audio symbol to listeners that *Monitor* was on the air—and to local stations, as well. It generally was played for 7 to 10 seconds, enough time for the stations to join, or rejoin, the network after playing their local news or commercials. When *Monitor* aired, the Beacon would be heard several times—at the beginning of each hour or half-hour, and at the mid-way point of each half-hour (when affiliates were given time to insert their own commercials).

Communicator Dave Garroway quickly took special note of the Beacon in the first hours of *Monitor's* premiere broadcast. After hearing it on the air, Garroway said: "There. Isn't that a mad noise? That's *Monitor's* trademark, and it will call your attention to the show most anytime you hear it." (12)

Listeners quickly learned that the Beacon meant *Monitor* was on the way. Even one of NBC's network competitors—in an effort to downplay the program's prospects—took note of it, calling the Beacon nothing more than "beeps and boops." (13)

As *Monitor's* June 12 debut approached, the program staff had grown to about 50 people. They, alone, would not have been enough to fill 40 consecutive hours of network broadcasting—so program producers and assignment editors began reaching out to NBC's radio affiliates, asking for ideas and, if possible, taped stories that could be aired on *Monitor.* Some of those local-station contributors would become the stuff of legend at NBC—local reporters who had the energy, enthusiasm and skill to put together memorable stories that would air on *Monitor.*

On Friday, June 10, NBC sent its affiliates a "fact sheet" about *Monitor:*

> *This Sunday 4 p.m., New York Time,* Monitor *takes over the airwaves. First hour: an hour-long simulcast on both the NBC Radio and NBC-TV networks; thereafter, seven hours of uninterrupted radio broadcasting.*
>
> Monitor *will be introduced to the public by Sylvester L. Weaver Jr., who will explain the new programming concept. Upon completion of the simulcast,* Monitor *will continue until midnight NYT with a potpourri of the best in news, information, service and entertainment. (14)*

The information sheet highlighted a few of the many features planned for that Sunday broadcast. Among them: an amazing number of live broadcasts from around the country and the world, including music from New York, Chicago and Los Angeles; mid-air reports from a TWA Constellation "equipped with a special *Monitor* transmitter"; and live news reports from London, Rome, Paris, Bonn, Istanbul, Tokyo, Capetown, Singapore, Montreal and "in other places wherever news is breaking."

Many celebrity interviews were planned, including Marilyn Monroe and Bob Hope; poet Carl Sandburg would be singing some of his favorite songs; live reports would come in from a Baptist church service in Columbia, South Carolina; from major-league baseball stadiums; and from the planet Jupiter (well, not exactly a live report—listeners would hear sounds from Jupiter).

Much more was planned both this coming Sunday and in future weeks on *Monitor*—and, the fact sheet said, NBC's affiliates could help out a lot:

"Remember, *Monitor* is only as good as you make it, so keep the suggestions and the tapes coming this way." (15)

On the same day NBC sent its fact sheet to its affiliates, Terrence O'Flaherty, the longtime radio-TV columnist for the *San Francisco Chronicle*, wrote about *Monitor:*

> *This weekend NBC radio will uncap an impressive new venture in broadcasting titled* Monitor. *It is expected to stimulate radio programming in the same manner that the NBC "Spectaculars" stimulated television. (16)*

Actually, *Monitor* had to stimulate NBC's radio programming—or else. Pat Weaver was rolling the dice—betting his radio network's future that *Monitor,* his revolutionary new type of programming—a true magazine of the air—would catch on with and perhaps even excite the American listening audience.

The stakes were monumental: If *Monitor* worked, NBC Radio could survive for a while longer in the age of television.

If it failed, NBC Radio—America's first radio network—might well become the first one to fold.

4

On the Air!

Sunday, June 12, 1955. A broadcasting revolution called *Monitor* was ready to spring from NBC's new Radio Central on the fifth floor of the RCA Building in midtown Manhattan, and you could have read all about it in the *New York Times*—if you knew where to look.

Not on the front page, of course. Radio programs rarely made Page 1 of the *Times*—unless they scared the daylights out of millions of individuals, as Orson Welles' *War of the Worlds* did on a Sunday night in October 1938, with a broadcast that convinced many Americans that Martians had invaded. That provoked such reaction that the *Times*—and lots of other newspapers—devoted many column inches to it on their front pages the following day.

On this particular Sunday in June of '55, the *Times* devoted its Page 1 to a story about a car that plunged into the crowd at the Le Mans auto race in Paris, killing 71 people; a report about President Eisenhower's commencement address at Penn State University, in which he proposed that the United States promote world progress by providing nuclear reactors to friendly foreign countries; and another one about how a cheaper hydrogen bomb was now possible.

Also making front-page news that day was word that shadow warfare continued in the Formosa Strait, that pressure for liberalizing East-West

33

trade was mounting and that United States diplomacy was entering one of its most critical stages since the start of the Cold War.

A small box on the lower-left part of the page contained several sports nuggets, including word that Nashua won the Belmont Stakes by nine lengths and that the Cleveland Indians had rallied to beat the Yankees, 7 to 6.

A box at the top of the page (next to the *Times'* logo) had a brief weather forecast (showers early, then partly cloudy). On the other side of the logo was the *Times'* slogan, "All the News That's Fit to Print." (1)

The *Times'* Section 2—its arts and entertainment section—featured advertisements heralding the upcoming June 23 opening of Disney's *Lady and the Tramp* movie. Currently playing in New York movie theaters were *Strategic Air Command* starring James Stewart and June Allyson and *The Seven Year Itch* starring Marilyn Monroe. On the Broadway stage, Karl Malden and Paul Newman were starring in *The Desperate Hours*. (2)

It was on Page 9 of Section 2 of that day's *Times* that you could find a two-paragraph story about what was about to take place that day in the world of radio:

> Monitor, *a new venture in network radio, makes its debut today. NBC is so proud of its new baby that it literally will show off* Monitor *by putting the first hour from 4 to 5 p.m. on both television and radio. The broadcast continues on radio until midnight tonight.*
>
> *Thereafter,* Monitor *will begin each Saturday at 8 a.m. and continue uninterrupted until Sunday midnight. The series will consist of all sorts of short features in addition to basic services such as news reports, time signals and weather information. Judging from NBC's plans,* Monitor *will contain most anything that can be crammed into a radio microphone within a forty-hour period. (3)*

To make sure that *Times* readers knew about *Monitor,* NBC purchased its own display advertisement in the Arts section. Headlined "Special Premiere," the ad showed a montage of eight photos arranged to form the figure of the world. Underneath, *Monitor's* new logo appeared in capital letters. Beneath the logo was the phrase "round the clock round the world, the new kind of radio listening."

The ad promised listeners they would hear, among other things, an interview with the pilot of the S.S. United States as he brought his vessel into New York Harbor; a jazz concert; informal chats with the cast of *Damn Yankees* backstage on Broadway; interviews with Helen Hayes, Mary Martin and George Abbott from France, discussing America's "Salute to France"; and "everything from a one-line joke to an unexpected news break."

The participants listed were Dave Garroway, John Cameron Swayze, Clifton Fadiman, Red Barber, Jim Fleming, Ben Grauer (an NBC announcer who had done many network programs), Walter Kiernan, Morgan Beatty and Frank Blair, whom the ad described as "favorites of radio and TV."

The ad urged readers to "listen today to the special *Monitor* premiere. And beginning next Saturday—wherever you are, whatever you're doing, go everywhere for 40 uninterrupted hours, with *Monitor.*"

That ad appeared next to the weekly TV program listings—in which NBC's Channel 4—WRCA-TV—was shown as having *Monitor* on the air from 4 to 5 p.m. (4)

Over on the radio listings page, *Monitor* was shown as airing from 4 p.m. to midnight on WRCA Radio. It was described as a "continuous program of news, sports, weather, music, entertainment and remote pick-ups from all parts of the world." More information was provided about what listeners could hear that afternoon and evening on *Monitor.*

Anyone reading or hearing about any of the hype or hoopla over *Monitor* in the days or hours before its debut may well have been wondering what in the world NBC Radio had up its sleeve.

At 4 p.m., listeners to that first Monitor broadcast found out.
This is how Mass Communication Professor Jim Wilson recounts that historic moment on June 12, 1955:

> *The second hand continued to click until it was straight up—the top of the hour—and for the first time, America heard the soon-to-be-familiar boop-and-beep sound of the* Monitor *Beacon. A moment later, announcer Ben Grauer proclaimed, "*Monitor! *Four p.m. Eastern Daylight Time; 20-hundred Greenwich Mean Time. This is* Monitor—*reporting the nation and the world."*
>
> *With that, Grauer introduced the President of NBC, Sylvester L. Weaver Jr., who welcomed the audience to this "premiere broadcast" of* Monitor, *"our new NBC weekend program" which is "for all of you wherever you are"—on the beach, in your car, etc. Weaver noted that the first hour of the radio program also was being televised by NBC-TV. He then said that they were going to "throw away the radio clock" and present "the radio pattern of the future" with a program containing news and features that would be as long or as short as they need to be.*
>
> *Weaver noted that* Monitor *would feature such personalities as Dave Garroway, Bob and Ray, Ben Grauer, NBC newsmen Morgan Beatty and Merrill Mueller, Walter Kiernan and Clifton Fadiman. He then introduced* Monitor's *executive producer Jim Fleming, who explained that the first hour of the broadcast would feature a "live" jazz concert from Southern California's Hermosa Beach, an inside look at San Quentin Prison in the northern part of that state, and an appearance by comedian Jerry Lewis, "filmed in the Catskills." It was also noted during the broadcast that* Monitor *had a transmitter aboard a flight from Idlewild*

Airport in New York to London and would also have a report from Istanbul, Turkey.

To begin the broadcast, communicator Dave Garroway gave some brief news headlines (from Bonn, German Chancellor Conrad Adenauer was flying to Washington; a labor dispute in Detroit; the Ku Klux Klan had held its first open meeting in three years and a crash at the Le Mans motor race in France had left 84 people dead.) Fleming told the audience that Monitor *was there when the Le Mans crash took place (acknowledging that it happened 22 hours earlier) and then introduced Raymond Baxter of the BBC, who offered comments on what happened. After the Baxter report, Fleming called in NBC newsman Frank Bourgholzer from Paris for an update on the story.*

After the news segment, Weaver returned to describe the Communication Center at NBC—what would be known around Monitor *as Radio Central—adding that it was something that tourists would enjoy seeing. At this point, they switched to comedians Bob and Ray for a skit of just such a tour, with one of the characters asking the tour guide, "Why are you televising a radio broadcast?"*

Garroway returned to switch the Monitor *broadcast to Hermosa Beach, California, for a "live" performance of Howard Rumsey's Lighthouse All Stars, joined in progress. When the first number was over, bassist Rumsey welcomed* Monitor *and served as host for the musical segment.*

The first broadcast of what would be an almost 20 year career for Monitor *was now underway. (5)*

Later that same hour, *Monitor* microphones (and cameras, this one time only) went to California's San Quentin Prison to interview inmates, to Chicago to hear (and see) the Art Van Damme quintet and to New

York's Idlewild Airport for the departure of TWA Flight 860 to London—the one carrying that special *Monitor* transmitter.

There was a pick-up of comedian Jerry Lewis at Brown's Hotel in the Catskills, talking about his latest movie with Dean Martin, *You're Never Too Young,* along with scenes and sound track from the movie. Another remote came from the Bucks County, Pennsylvania, playhouse for a dress rehearsal of Victor Jory's play, *The Fairly Fortunate;* and yet another pick-up took place with double-talk artist Al Kelly, interviewing baseball fans at Hurley and Davies Tavern in New York.

And there was the noise made by an oyster.

All that, in *Monitor's* first hour. (6)

The television simulcast ended at 5 p.m., putting *Monitor* into the position it would occupy for the rest of its broadcast life—as a radio (only) program. The pace generated in that first hour hardly slackened in the next seven.

News broadcasts were positioned at the top of each hour, followed by more live dance bands; a book review; an evaluation of Indian Prime Minister Nehru; a live remote from a ceremony in Scotland; several return visits to San Quentin Prison; live music from Nick's Tavern in New York; and interviews with Mary Martin, Helen Hayes, Marilyn Monroe and others.

Additionally, there was a live pick-up of poet Carl Sandburg receiving the Boston Arts Festival annual award; numerous mid-air reports from that TWA flight winging its way across the Atlantic; an interview with Harvard University President Dr. Nathan Pusey; and comedian Victor Borge interviewing best-selling author Louis Bromfield on how to grow and eat food properly.

There was a three-way pick-up from Bonn, Germany; Washington, D.C. and New York on the German chancellor's proposed trip to Moscow; a radio signal from the planet Jupiter, 400 million miles from Radio Central; and an interview with pianist Crazy Otto from a Berlin beer hall.

Monitor visited the Detroit Zoo's lion house; provided numerous baseball updates; and took listeners to hear the congregation of a Baptist church in Columbia, South Carolina, sing hymns.

Additionally, Bob and Ray provided comedy routines throughout the evening; "Miss Monitor" gave her provocative weather forecasts and Henry Morgan gave his pronouncements on the evening's TV shows. (7)

In other words, *Monitor* had given listeners that "kaleidoscopic phantasmagoria" that Pat Weaver had promised almost three months earlier.

Monitor had, with an amazing amount of advance publicity, promised to keep listeners "in instantaneous touch with everything interesting or entertaining anywhere in the world." There was no doubt that the premiere program attempted to do just that. But would listeners—and critics—buy into it?

The critics weighed in first. Jack Gould, the *New York Times* media observer, started his column the next day this way:

> *Sylvester L. (Pat) Weaver Jr., broadcasting's most unpredictable president, started something yesterday over his National Broadcasting Company's radio network. Just what it is, however, he may be the only man to know for a while.*

Then Gould called *Monitor* a cousin of Weaver's *Today, Home* and *Tonight* shows—"something of an electronic grab-bag, designed to keep a listener guessing as to what's coming next." Gould said the premiere's "pickings were mixed":

> *In part, Monitor was new and different, engendering a radio equivalent of the narcotic TV quality that keeps a viewer watching, for instance, Steve Allen. A listener was curious to know what would happen next. In part, Monitor was familiar NBC radio in a slightly different garb.*

Gould described *Monitor*'s 4 p.m. start as "bizarre" because, he said, the two media broadcasting it—radio and TV—got tangled up "to produce a hodge-podge." He said more attention was paid to the TV aspect than to the radio part, but acknowledged that "undoubtedly Mr. Weaver achieved his objective of calling attention by means of TV to the fact that there still is sound broadcasting."

At 5 p.m., after the TV simulcast ended, *Monitor* began to hit its stride, Gould said, adding that it was this stretch "that had the most pace—a liveliness and an uncertainty that held the listener's attention." He added that as the program's hours ran on, "the problem of repetition began to assert itself," as the national news began at the top of each hour and updates on the same features began showing up at regular intervals.

Gould said that Garroway "is not the best of interviewers, as was evident in his talk with Marilyn Monroe." And Gould said that the "short-wave pick-ups, not too many of which worked very well, lost a good deal of their value when nobody had anything very special to say."

And Gould became the first of many who would note the presence of "Miss Monitor":

> *A big, if unidentified, hit of* Monitor *was a young lady who delivered weather reports for just about every city in the world except New York. She made the report sound like an irresistible invitation to an unforgettable evening.*

And the critic ended on a positive note:

> Monitor *has such a flexible format that in the weekends to come Mr. Weaver will be able to experiment to his heart's delight. And if his past accomplishments are a criterion, he will. Which is perhaps the best guarantee that at long last network radio is going to receive a shot in the arm. (8)*

Time magazine weighed in with a highly positive review that first described NBC's problem that led to *Monitor:* "For the past six years, radio-network income has plummeted to catastrophic depths and the network hardest hit has been NBC. To get out of the red, NBC is trying *Monitor*, a 40-hour, nonstop, weekend radio show."

And *Time* was impressed, saying that *Monitor* "took its listeners on the kind of joy ride that led Pat Weaver to describe his brain child as a 'kaleidoscopic phantasmagoria.'" After describing a few of the program segments, including the oyster sounds, *Time* concluded: "With all the facilities of the network thrown its way, *Monitor,* a natural rover built for speed, proved first time out that it had variety, imagination, a sense of humor and an oyster bed full of gimmicks." (9)

Newsweek was even more impressed. Its review began by noting that "in the feverish world of broadcasting, the dreams of NBC president Sylvester (Pat) Weaver are generally conceded to be the biggest and best around. They also have a disconcerting habit of coming true."

> *Last week in a $150,000 studio on the fifth floor of Rockefeller Center in New York, behind a vast expanse of plate glass and in the midst of myriad dials, plugs, knobs, switches and pale apple green walls, still another Weaver dream materialized. Called* Monitor, *it promised to be by all odds the longest and most frenetic radio program in history.*

Monitor had, *Newsweek* continued, "enough interesting, exasperating, and mysterious aural sensations to bear out producer Jim Fleming's boast that *Monitor* would bring its audience 'everything important, entertaining or interesting that is happening anywhere.'"

Newsweek described a few of the more exotic remotes and features and concluded, "After it was all over, there was no question that *Monitor* was startlingly different and grandiosely ambitious." (10)

Printers' Ink magazine weighed in with an encouraging review about *Monitor:*

> *It offers a flexible design for network spot sales and programming chock full of personalities and remote events that affiliates*

can stack against music-news-weather formats of independent stations—formats that for audience pull are hard for networks to top these days.

Monitor *represents the principal experiment with new programing that is current in radio. It's NBC's way of trying to find the correct formula for radio in the TV era. For advertisers, the* Monitor *format sets up maximum opportunity for short commercials. For listeners, it presents new scope in world coverage and new variety of format.*

The magazine said that, based on the Sunday preview, "It's safe to presume that *Monitor* will do a competent job on world and national news." The magazine also took special note of a certain weather forecaster, saying that "'Miss Monitor' (voice over soft music on weather reports around the world) makes 41 degrees and cloudy in Moscow seem like sultry summer weather." (11)

Broadcasting-Telecasting magazine, the so-called "bible" of the broadcast industry, also had positive things to say about *Monitor:*

NBC has cast asunder the conventional "radio clock" for better or worse—probably better—with the premiere of its Monitor *weekend network programming service. Whether it will find it profitable to keep on "going places and doing things" in the months ahead remains to be determined. But* Monitor *seems to have made a promising start with its new concept of radio service for the casual listeners at home, on the road, at the beach. Certainly the ingredients are there—an intricate facilities setup and a goodly assortment of "communicators," plus a flexible format.*

The magazine gave particular credit to Clifton Fadiman and Dave Garroway, "who distinguished themselves as communicators in the premiere," along with producer Jim Fleming. Then it discussed *Monitor's* possible future: "In the end, its potential lies in getting the casual listener to tune in frequently rather than continuously over a 40-hour weekend spread. " (12)

So with a few negatives and many more positives, reviewers gave *Monitor* two-thumbs up for its innovation, energy and freshness. Many questions remained, however. Could *Monitor* maintain the frenetic pace of its opening weekend? Could it remain fresh weekend after 40-hour weekend? Would listeners "buy into" the concept? Would advertisers who had purchased commercials on the premiere program stay on board, and would others join them?

Monitor's eight-hour premiere had passed its first tests with critics. Now the program had to settle in for the long haul, and find enough interesting, exciting and entertaining people, places and things to fill up weekend after weekend of broadcasting, starting the following Saturday at 8 a.m.

5

"Going Places and Doing Things"

The advertisement NBC Radio bought in the *New York Times* on Friday, June 17, 1955—the day before *Monitor's* first full 40-hour weekend on the air—promised readers that if they listened, they would "go everywhere this weekend with *Monitor*." The ad also called the program "the new kind of radio listening" and used the slogan, "'round the clock 'round the world, hear it all on *Monitor*." (1)

From its first moments on the air, *Monitor* tried mightily to live up to those slogans and another one that promised listeners they'd be "going places and doing things" each weekend. Many of those places and things would be unusual, others would be important and still others would be wacky. That was what Pat Weaver wanted—a program that anyone, anywhere, could tune into anytime and find something of interest.

On that first "full" weekend of *Monitor* on June 18 and 19, 1955, listeners had their choice of a wide array of options. That weekend, *Monitor* had, among other things, live remote pick-ups of dance orchestras in New York, Chicago and Los Angeles; a match race between two horses; segments from the National Open Golf Tournament in San Francisco; the Army's one millionth parachute jump over Fort Bragg, North Carolina; a civil defense evacuation test from Reading, Pennsylvania; and the Grand Ole Opry from Nashville, Tennessee (a regular Saturday night live pick-up for years on *Monitor*).

In addition, of course, there were up-to-the-minute news reports, including a *Monitor* exclusive: the first American radio broadcast with Soviet Foreign Minister V.M. Molotov when he arrived that Sunday in San Francisco for the United Nations' 10th anniversary conference. "Mr. Molotov was about to leave the train terminal when (NBC news reporter Pauline) Frederick tapped on the window of his car and recorded—for use on NBC's *Monitor* show about an hour later—a brief interview in which he expressed his thanks for the welcome extended to the Soviet Union delegates." (2)

Monitor's "gimmicks" were also on hand: Bob and Ray provided live comedy routines throughout the weekend; and "Miss Monitor" gave her unusual weather forecasts, also all weekend long. In the newspaper listing, no times were given for any of these events. (3)

That changed, in part, the following weekend, June 25 and 26, when the radio listings showed that *Monitor* would have live remote pick-ups on Saturday from speedboat races in Detroit at 12:35, 1:05, 3:55 and 6:05 p.m. and from the AAU track and field championships from Boulder, Colorado, at 5:20, 6:50 and 7:40 p.m. Also planned that day: live dance music from various parts of the nation at unspecified time periods and interviews with Bob Hope, Dinah Shore and Gloria Graham. (4)

The following day, on Sunday, *Monitor* had live remotes from a camel auction in Casablanca; a report on juvenile delinquency from Washington, D.C.; Air Force exercises in Western Europe; President Eisenhower fishing in Maine; and a motion picture company on location in Kansas. (5)

It would be this way weekend after weekend for years—a wide variety of remotes from anywhere in the world on practically any topic imaginable. *Monitor's* staff and the stringers—independent reporters from NBC affiliates—who contributed reports to the show would go anywhere to provide material for the broadcast. At least in the beginning, and for a few years after that, "money was no object," according to a long-time *Monitor* producer. (6)

On Saturday, July 2, 1955, *Monitor's* live pick-ups included a visit to the Voice of America's floating relay station in the Mediterranean; to a buffalo drive down the old Santa Fe Trail; to the Women's National Open Golf Tournament in Wichita, Kansas; and to the Wimbledon Tennis Championships in England. (7)

The following day, *Monitor* had live broadcasts from an undersea exploration of a Confederate blockade runner that went down off Long Island in 1861. But the day's biggest remotes came from New Boston, New Hampshire, where a typical old-fashioned Fourth of July celebration was in progress. The only atypical aspect of it was, according to the *New York Times*, the fact that "the celebration will be a day early, and that's because NBC asked to have it advanced for (*Monitor*)." (8)

Guests on *Monitor* that weekend included entertainers Shirley Jones, Gordon MacRae, Harry Belafonte, Eddie Fisher, Humphrey Bogart, Jackie Gleason and Sammy Davis Jr. (9)

Monitor apparently had so impressed the *New York Times* that on Sunday, July 10, the newspaper printed a short story commemorating the program's fourth weekend on the air. It was accompanied by four pictures of *Monitor's* men and women in action, including engineers at *Monitor's* big control board in Radio Central; several other engineers surrounding turntables; Capi Petrash, who was in charge of bringing in broadcasts from "remote points in many foreign countries"; and a picture of *Monitor* communicators Dave Garroway, Morgan Beatty, Walter Kiernan and Clifton Fadiman, all seated around a table in the studio. (10)

Week by week that first summer, *Monitor* picked up the pace of its broadcasts, seemingly going to an increasing number of places and doing an increasing number of things each Saturday and Sunday. The weekend of September 10 and 11 proves the point: On Saturday, the live remotes included two from the Pentagon Communications Center in Washington, D.C.; from an amusement park ride; from the Automation Show in Chicago; from a boat party in Myrtle Beach, South Carolina; from an elephant party in San Francisco; from the Green Cheese Festival in Monroe, Wisconsin; from the Discovery Handicap horse race; from the Cavalcade of Golf and the National Tennis Singles Tournament.

There was more, including live reports on sea lions; another on marlin fishing; one from the Kansas City zoo; and a live remote from the Grand Ole Opry's Saturday night party from Nashville, Tennessee.

Guests on *Monitor* that day—just that one day—included entertainers Frank Sinatra, Perry Como, Pearl Bailey, Mary Martin, Steve Allen, Lena Horne and Dick Powell and songwriters Sammy Cahn and Jimmy Van Heusen. (11)

The next day, *Monitor* kept up this blistering pace by having live remotes from the Barnum and Bailey Circus; the Cavalcade of Golf Tournament; a Forest Hills Tennis Tournament; an Army language school in San Francisco; a dog show; a square dance; a polar laboratory in Cleveland; a training class for paraplegics at Walter Reed Hospital; a Chinese opera house; a shrimp fleet; and a re-enactment of the Fort McHenry bombardment.

Guests that Sunday included Helen Hayes, Gene Kelly, Esther Williams, Ethel Barrymore, Perry Como, Frank de Vol, Pee Wee Erwin and a snake charmer from India. (12)

In those early days of *Monitor*, it seemed that if anything was interesting—no matter what or where it was—it was on *Monitor*. Take, for example, the first weekend of October 1955, when *Monitor's* live remotes included visits to a "building bee" in Binghamton, New York; a ride on a Los Angeles streetcar; an interview with a New York Madison Avenue bus driver; an auction of old automobiles in Claremore, Oklahoma; the commissioning of the aircraft carrier Forrestal in Portsmouth, Virginia; the construction of the Nyack-Terrytown bridge; a San Francisco arts festival; a visit to the New York Headache Clinic; and a look at the autumnal equinox from a planetarium. Guests that weekend included Maurice Chevalier, Jean Simmons, Milton Berle, John Wayne, Esther Williams, Myron Cohen, Jessica Tandy, Hume Cronyn, Peggy Lee, Herb Shriner, Ted Lewis and the late Enrico Caruso's cook. (13)

A *Monitor* staple–at least in the program's early years–was the live remote pick-up of big-band music. Such remotes were expensive—and complicated–to produce, but they were plentiful in the first months of the program.

For example, on Saturday, Oct. 8, 1955, *Monitor's* band-remote schedule included 11 pick-ups from nightclubs in New York City, Chicago, Los Angeles and Dearborn, Michigan. The following day, *Monitor* "went live" with nine band remotes from those same cities. Generally, the program's remotes each ran from six to 15 minutes. They featured such "big names" as George Shearing, Stan Kenton, Les Elgart, Pee Wee Irwin, Wilbur De Paris and others.

As *Monitor's* format changed over time, the band remotes gradually faded away, replaced by more and more "canned" music.

Over the years, *Monitor* went to the ends of the Earth to get the interesting, the unusual—even the wacky—events. *Monitor* correspondents once waited three days and nights in the wilds of New Zealand to deliver the "cheep" of a nesting kiwi bird. *Monitor* went on a 26-week African safari with famed radio writer Arch Oboler, whose assignment was to bring back the snap of a crocodile's jaws from Lake Victoria and the pound of antelopes' hooves.

Monitor staffers once tracked down entertainer Danny Kaye to a Finnish bath in Helsinki. There, he was interviewed to the sounds of moans, slaps and groans.

Monitor also featured the sounds of mating shrimp and of worms cutting the roots of corn. A *Monitor* reporter breathlessly made his first parachute jump. Another made a ride on a giant roller-coaster and passed out during her report. Yet another reported on whales breathing. One *Monitor* interview featured Winston Churchill Mulholland—a talking myna bird.

Many of *Monitor's* feature reports, at least in the early days of the program, were produced by "stringers." One of them was Don Kennedy, who was a frequent contributor to the program:

> *Having just been released from the Army and only earning*
> *$75 a week as a booth announcer for WSB-TV (in Atlanta),*

there wasn't much money available, but I took a chance and bought a portable $299 Magnecord tape recorder from a mail-order house on time payments. Another Army buddy and extremely talented announcer, Harlee Branch, was a native Atlantan and suggested some subjects, among them golf great Bobby Jones.

I found Jones in a law office in downtown Atlanta and also found my first acceptance by Monitor *for that interview. I painstakingly edited it down to the required three minutes or less, using regular Scotch tape, for I'm not sure splicing tape had yet been introduced.*

It was fascinating to hear the interview come back on WSB Radio in Atlanta, for even though I thought my editing had pared the interview to the absolute bone while still keeping some meaning, the Monitor *editor cut it down still more, still retaining the flavor of the interview and making it far superior to my original submission. (14)*

Kennedy remembers producing a *Monitor* feature about a 105-year old lady who recalled her parents talking about the Civil War and another about a so-called "Goat Man," an evangelist who traveled from New England to Florida each year on a cart pulled by several goats. One of Kennedy's more unusual efforts involved a trip to Georgia's Stone Mountain to recreate the rescue of a dog that had fallen down the steep side of the 900-foot granite rock, but had been saved from death by landing on a scaffold left there years earlier by carvers on the mountain:

There had, in fact, been a dog rescued by a resident of the town of Stone Mountain a few weeks earlier, but given the difficulty in getting up the mountain in time to actually record such a rescue was, in practical terms, not possible, so we faked it.

*Elias Nour was known for his rescue work, and despite his
40-ish age, was known in those parts as "The Old Man of the
Mountain." Since the old Magnecorder had to be plugged in,
we tapped into an AC outlet in a shack that was at the base of
a red aircraft warning light.*

*Then Elias went back down the mountain, drove his Jeep up
as I described his arrival and set the scene, then interviewed
him as his helpers unloaded rope and hooks to begin the
descent down the steep side of the mountain. He described the
call about the "dog being stranded" and the rescue technique
and left the mic to get to the top of the carving where the help-
less dog was presumably awaiting human intervention.
That was the first three-minute part. The second, to be aired
an hour later, was an interview with Mr. Nour as he theoret-
ically appeared from below, holding the hapless hound whom
he described as "not making a sound as yet." (15)*

During those early years, *Monitor's* staff members were augmented by
about 150 stringers around the world. Their "beats" included everything,
and their common goal was to get the best, most interesting and most
unusual sounds possible on the air. "If we cover a sheep-shearing in
Australia," said *Monitor* assignment editor Burroughs Prince, "I want to
hear the sound of the shears and the wool falling." (16)

"The world is *Monitor's* oyster," is how one newspaper reporter would
describe the program on its 11th anniversary. It fit.

Of course there were the planned events, and then there was "breaking
news"—those unplanned stories about events of national or worldwide
importance—that were frequently a part of *Monitor's* weekend. Veteran
NBC announcer Ben Grauer became a "communicator" on *Monitor* in
September 1955, and as luck would have it, his first Sunday on the air featured a major newsbreak:

> *I started the 2 o'clock (*Monitor*) with a five-minute newscast*
> *at the top of the thing, and then there was a spot of some kind,*
> *I forget what, and (co-host Frank Gallop) cut in and said,*
> *"Ben, there's word from the newsroom that something impor-*
> *tant's happening in Argentina," and they shoved a brief at me,*
> *a bulletin, and I made the announcement and switched to*
> *Argentina, to Buenos Aires, where the NBC man (was)*
> *revealing the first breaking news that (Argentine dictator*
> *Juan) Peron was being...thrown out. (17)*

Monitor producer Elliot "Bud" Drake—who became a staff member a year or so after the program went on the air and stayed almost to the end—recalls one memorable night that he considers the most exciting broadcast he ever had on the show. It was Sunday night, September 30, 1962, when James Meredith tried to become the first black student at the University of Mississippi. Riots broke out.

Drake's host on that Sunday night *Monitor* segment was NBC newsman Frank McGee. Drake says just before the 7 p.m. start of the show, "McGee came into the control room and said, 'Bud, throw the whole show out.'"

The entire three-hour broadcast was then devoted to live reports from several NBC correspondents in Mississippi. McGee ad-libbed most of the three-hours. Nearly 40 years after the event, Drake vividly recalls that night on *Monitor*:

> *We were so far ahead of what was happening. We had three*
> *people down there (in Mississippi), phoning in stories as they*
> *happened. The Associated Press and United Press International*
> *were listening to our show, so as we reported stuff, all of a sud-*
> *den it would appear on AP. There was so much going on. It was*
> *a classic show. (18)*

Indeed it was. *Monitor* won a Peabody Award for its coverage from Mississippi that night.

From the start, interviews with all kinds of people were a staple of *Monitor*. The biggest names from the world of entertainment and politics would make their way to Radio Central for either live or taped interviews—but *Monitor* microphones would also pick up interviews from those who may not have been famous but who had unusual jobs or hobbies.

One of communicator Dave Garroway's most famous *Monitor* interviews was one of his first, with Hollywood superstar Marilyn Monroe:

GARROWAY: Wonder if I'm scared of you. Are most men scared of you? I'm not sure whether I should be frightened of you or not.

MONROE: No, nobody's scared of me.

GARROWAY: I don't know. I bet a lot of guys are scared of you, though, because you're such an institution, really you are, you're kind of a national possession. Do you feel that you belong to the nation as a whole?

MONROE: I don't know quite what you mean by that. I live here.

GARROWAY: (LAUGHING) That'll do it very nicely. I hear that you moved into New York City to live. Is this so?

MONROE: Yes, this will be my home from now on, that is, until I retire, and when I retire, I'm going to retire to Brooklyn. (19)

Garroway's Sunday night *Monitor* segment—which he would host until 1961—became known for its frequent interviews with the famous and not-so famous. Often those guests would be at Radio Central live; but many times, the interviews would be on tape.

And sometimes those taped interviews that Garroway seemed to be doing had, in reality, been done by other NBC staffers who had talked with the person earlier. The staffer's questions would then be edited out of the conversation, and those same questions would be read by Garroway, often live, to introduce the respondent's taped answer.

The process is known as a "stop-tape" interview. One of those who often did interviews that would be "fronted" by Garroway at Radio Central was NBC newsman John Chancellor. He would later, of course, become anchor of *NBC Nightly News* on television—but in the mid-1950s, he was a radio reporter in Chicago who was often assigned to get interviews for the "big man," Garroway, in New York:

> *We had interviews that were presented as interviews that Dave Garroway did. And for my sins I got to do a lot of these interviews, and Garroway would ask the questions and they would play the tape of the answers I got from people. And my voice never appeared.*
>
> *And I got a call from New York one day, saying the interviews are fine, but they're not personal enough. And I said, "What do you mean, personal?" And they said, "Well, have the people begin the answers with, 'Well, Dave.'"*
>
> *So I tried this for a week or two and interviewed some people, and they kept forgetting to say, "Well, Dave." So I got a sign printed that said, "Dave" and hung it around my neck. And in asking questions, I would point as they thought of the answer to "Dave." And I guess we had the highest "Well, Dave" rate at the network. (20)*

One of Garroway's most poignant interviews on *Monitor*—one that he actually did, since the guest was live at Radio Central—was with entertainment great Eddie Cantor, a star of vaudeville, film and radio. Cantor's career had been interrupted four years earlier by a heart attack. Garroway asked him whether vaudeville was demanding, a kind of survival test of the wittiest. Cantor's response:

> *As a matter of fact, it was not a grind. It was pretty easy. We like to think that it was tough. These are the hard days. The early days were easy because, let's find out what vaudeville*

was. Small-time vaudeville was kindergarten. Then you grad-
uated into big-time vaudeville, which was grammar school.
Then you went into a Broadway show, which was high school.
And you got in with Ziegfeld, you were in the university.
Today there is no kindergarten. There is no grammar school.
There is no high school. You go immediately on television,
which is your university. There's no place to break in. You
might go to some nightclubs; you might go to some Catskill
Mountain resorts; but actually, bing! There you are, and you
play to more people in one night, in radio and on television,
than we played sometimes in a lifetime.
But the old days were the nice days, leisurely days, comfortable
days. Call it the horse-and-buggy period if you like, but there
was something…warm and sentimental, and no great rush.
And no heart attacks. No heart attacks. (21)

Monitor had thousands of interviews on the air during the life of the
show. Another that stands out was one that host Frank McGee did with
civil rights leader Martin Luther King Jr. on one of McGee's Sunday night
programs.

McGEE: I know that your home has been dynamited and
that you have had threats made against your life on many
occasions, and these are not idle gestures as the fate of Medgar
Evers (a civil rights leader assassinated in 1963) in
Mississippi so tragically demonstrates. I am certain you have
given some thought to this and I would like to know what
your feelings on this are.
KING: Yes, I have given thought to this. And I go on with the
feeling that this is a righteous cause, and that we will have to
suffer in this cause, and that if physical death is the price that
some must pay, if it's the price that I must pay to free my chil-
dren and the children of my brothers and sisters and my white

*brothers from a permanent psychological death, then nothing
can be more redemptive.
I have always believed that unearned suffering is redemptive,
and if a man has not discovered something so dear and so pre-
cious that he will die for it, then he doesn't have much to live
for...
If I fall in this cause, then I think it will certainly be something worthy of falling in, and something worthy of all those
who engage in this struggle. (22)*

King was assassinated in Memphis, Tennessee, in April 1968.

It wasn't just the famous who made it on *Monitor's* air. In 1965, a 12-year old girl from Illinois had her wish fulfilled, thanks to *Monitor.* She had written to President Johnson, asking for his photograph, explaining how she had missed the chance to get his picture during a campaign stop in Illinois.

A few days later, she received that autographed picture from the President and his personal invitation to attend his inauguration for a new term in 1965.

During the course of the *Monitor* report, the girl's father said that the family could not afford to travel to Washington for the inauguration. Immediately after the interview aired on *Monitor,* NBC's switchboards were flooded with offers that allowed them to make the trip.

Another *Monitor* report brought a doctor to a Wisconsin town that was about to lose its only physician. After hearing the *Monitor* story, another doctor drove to the small town and replaced the departing physician.

Monitor had an abundance of "firsts" and "exclusives." In 1964, the program had the first interview with U.S. Surgeon General Luther Terry after he released his report on the dangers of smoking. Later that year, *Monitor* had the first eyewitness report from Anchorage, Alaska, which had just been struck by a devastating earthquake.

In order to showcase some of its reports, *Monitor* created a feature called "Ring Around the World." Foreign correspondents covering, for example, a Presidential visit overseas or a foreign disaster, would have their stories introduced with that title and a distinctive audio sounder.

In addition to covering virtually anything and everything that was important, interesting or unusual in the world, *Monitor* often put together special reports on themed broadcasts.

One of those series aired in the early 1960s. It was called the "Date Special" and generally aired on the Sunday night *Monitor* segments hosted during those years by Frank McGee and, later, Frank Blair. "Date Specials" were segments of varying lengths highlighting historic events that took place on the date the segments aired. For example, the "Date Special" that McGee anchored on Sunday night, March 11, 1962, began this way:

McGEE (WITH MUSIC IN BACKGROUND): March 11th. A portentous date in any year. Not quite winter and not yet spring. The blizzard of 1888 began on this date. A wild, cosmic mocking of the warm sun that had chilled down on the East two days before.

March 11th, 1962, today. Snow, deep and uncongenial, lies thick over the Rockies. A still-bitter wind whips along Michigan Boulevard. But the change is coming. Deep-down stirrings in the Earth, subtle and silent. And a year ago tonight, the same conspiracy was afoot. Five years ago, it was the same. Twelve years. Twelve years ago tonight, March 11th it was, 1950, snow fell that night over the Great Lakes. There was a chilly wind in the Ohio and Upper Mississippi valleys. But spring was on the way.

The New York Times *for that date advertised women's sailor hats. Straw they were, and just the thing for Easter. You could get one with rayon-velvet facing for $19.95. If you wanted a garland of fruit, it cost $25.*

*Winter wheat was growing green in the fertile belt that
stretches northward from the Black Sea to the Ukraine. And
Soviet premier Molotov said that day that the Russian people
would not be frightened by the threat of a hydrogen bomb
because in his words, "It does not exist."*
*And in this country, we were hearing a new name and a new
voice. A harsh, accusing voice. It belonged to the junior senator from Wisconsin. His name was Joseph R. McCarthy. (23)*

What followed was a sound bite from McCarthy, who, as he often did
in the early 1950s, accused someone in government of harboring
Communist leanings. Then McGee discussed the Korean War and introduced sound bites involving that conflict. Finally he introduced the top
musical hit of 1950, the year the Korean War started. It was *How Much Is
That Doggie in the Window?* The "Date Special" ended this way:

*McGEE: March 11th, 1950. March 11, 1962. And each of
us has a rendezvous with another spring. Deep stirrings under
the Earth tonight. The sun's rising just a little higher each day
and lingering just a little longer. And 12 years from now, we
can look back at this spring, and know, surely, what we cannot know tonight: What was chaff and what was wheat,
where we were wise, and wherein foolish.*

The entire segment lasted eight minutes.

Occasionally, to dramatize events happening on a particular date, the
specials would involve actors who would read certain lines. Longtime
Monitor producer-director Bud Drake produced most of the "Date
Specials." Most of them were read live by the *Monitor* host of the evening.

Over the years, *Monitor* frequently would devote entire half-hour or
hour segments to events or people of special importance. One such segment aired on Sunday night, March 22, 1964, when McGee interviewed

legendary network radio newscaster Raymond Gram Swing, who had just written his autobiography.

> *McGEE: Good evening. This is Frank McGee, back with a special half-hour that is, we think, likely to stir the memories of hundreds of thousands of* Monitor *listeners. Do you recognize this voice?*
> *SWING: Good evening. I think it's worth reporting at length on the reaction of the United States to Mr. Chamberlain's promise of help to Poland. The Chamberlain pronouncements are understood as bringing a momentous and historic change to British policy…McGEE: That was Raymond Gram Swing, who throughout the '30s and '40s, was one of the country's, indeed one of the world's, foremost radio commentators. And what you heard him say in that excerpt of a broadcast 25 years ago over NBC was typical of what he always had to say…Well, Raymond Swing…will be 77 this week. His book of personal memoirs, appropriately called* Good Evening, *will be out, and many of his friends are gathering in New York to honor him.*

McGee and Swing talked about then-current world events and leaders and the difficulties those leaders had in keeping world peace. They also talked about what Swing considered the most important domestic question facing the United States in 1964: civil rights for Black Americans.

> *SWING: We now have an obligation to fulfill the promises of the Constitution to 10 percent of the population…We have been putting it off, putting it off year after year, decade after decade, and now the time has come for this promise to be fulfilled.*
> *McGEE: Why do you think the time has come now? Why this particular time?*

SWING: Because the breath of liberty is being breathed all over the world...and we can't very well be the leaders of that if we have not given real equality to members of the American family. (24)

Especially in its early years, *Monitor* often broke away from its "going places and doing things" pattern to "lighten up" an hour with a salute to a famous entertainer, particularly on that individual's birthday. Comedian Groucho Marx was the subject of one such hour-long salute hosted by Jim Lowe; fellow comedian George Burns was featured in another salute hosted by Gene Rayburn.

Perhaps the most poignant of these hours aired on Sunday, December 15, 1963. *Monitor* host Barry Nelson began it this way:

NELSON: This is Monitor *'63. I'm Barry Nelson. On Wednesday of this past week, as he ended a press conference that was broadcast on NBC News, Frank Sinatra added these words:*
SINATRA: Tomorrow is my birthday, and it's probably the best birthday I've ever had.
NELSON: The reason for his happiness on this particular birthday—the safe return of his kidnapped son, Frank Jr. And so, on Thursday, December 12th, Frank Sinatra celebrated his birthday in the company of his family and close friends. Today, the alleged kidnappers were arrested by the FBI.
With this resolution of what might have been a tragic situation, Monitor *is pleased to present, as previously planned, a special birthday salute to one of the greatest entertainers of our time, Frank Sinatra.*
In the hour ahead, we'll hear him talk candidly about many aspects of his career. We'll hear from Frank Sinatra Jr. and how he feels about his famous father. (25)

Ten years later—almost to the exact day of this *Monitor* salute to his father—Frank Sinatra Jr. became a *Monitor* guest host and talked about how he felt about his still-famous dad.

While *Monitor* prided itself on being on top of the day's news, the program was not averse to having fun. Drake, who began work on the show in 1956, recalls that his first chore was to pull together an "epic contest" called 'the most beautiful voice in America":

> *Somebody said, "Oh, what a wonderful idea. All our affiliates will come in on it, and we'll sell RCA equipment to the affiliates, and the affiliates will go out and record all these voices." And we never dreamed the harvest that we were going to reap. Because we were just inundated with tape from all over the country. It just got so big.*
>
> *I had to pull this thing together for 13 weeks and sort out all these voices. And at the end of this whole epic procedure, we ended up with five contest winners. And I was home in bed, sound asleep, in the middle of the night, and the phone rang, and it was the NBC operator. And she said, "Mr. Drake, we have your contest winner in Las Vegas. And they're not ready to accommodate them."*
>
> *And I said, "Good Lord, we never gave Las Vegas as a prize on the contest." And I called another guy who had arranged all the prizes on the contest, and I said, "Did we give Las Vegas?" And he said, "No."*
>
> *And I said, "Well, one of our winners is in Las Vegas. What are we going to do?" And he said, "Go back to sleep. I'll take care of everything."*
>
> *Somehow or other, he did. And it turned out that, early on, in all the literature about the contest, we HAD offered this as speculatively. But we had never promised it. And the KGU*

*(Radio) contest winner from Honolulu had been flown into
Las Vegas for a long week. And we covered it, of course. (26)*

In *Monitor's* first few years, the program often aired live remotes from
big bands across the United States. Those remotes were not only considered
interesting listening for the audience—they sometimes served another pur-
pose for the *Monitor* staff. Charles Garment, a long-time *Monitor* writer,
remembers that during the Saturday night segments he worked on, producer Murray Burnett enjoyed the remotes for personal reasons:

> *Murray would make sure the production assistants would set
> up the program around the band remote, which usually ran
> 15 to 18 minutes, and try to get it surrounded by taped mate-
> rial so the (*Monitor*) crew could get half an hour off and go
> play gin rummy or poker in the offices below the studio.
> It was that kind of atmosphere. A bunch of wacko characters
> who had a great time. We did everything in a free-swinging
> way. It was great fun. (27)*

As was often the case with live programming—and is still the case
today—if anything could go wrong, it did. Former *Monitor* engineer Bob
Dreier remembers one particular band remote:

> *One Saturday evening I was assigned to do the nemo (remote)
> at the Hotel Roosevelt where the Guy Lombardo orchestra
> held court. It was an easy nemo. The biggest mistake an engi-
> neer could make would be to show up at the wrong hotel; the
> Lombardo band was "self balancing." Set up three mics—one
> in front of the saxes which doubled as the announce mic and
> vocalist, one near the piano and one covering the bass fiddle
> for bottom. The brass took care of itself.
> Once you went on the air you sat back, set the initial levels
> and Lombardo did the rest. It was that simple.
> One particular Saturday night the NBC staff announcer*

assigned to the nemo got the brilliant idea that he would give Monitor *a slightly different version of the half-hour show. What was this brainstorm?*

He decided that he would take the announce mic out into the dance floor and talk to the old-timers who were doing their waltz. I said to him, "No way, Jose! The mic stays put in front of the saxes." Why? (This was the days before wireless microphones.) Simply because if he took the mic onto the dance floor and some senior tripped over the cable, NBC would be sued until the cows came home for big bucks. Big liability! He didn't want to listen. So I asked him once again NOT to do this, Monitor *or no* Monitor. *It was just too risky. It fell on deaf ears. The fact that I would lose the mic for the saxes and brass were nothing compared to the pending legal liability. I got on the engineering line and talked to the master control director and said that there would be no nemo tonight from the Hotel Roosevelt. "Hey, what's going on?" they wanted to know. So I explained to them what the scenario would be, and it's getting close to airtime. So* Monitor *went a different route. On Monday I get called into the front office to answer—"how come?" I explained the situation. They called up to legal and the answer came down: "The engineer made the correct response." Wheeeeew—off the hook. That was the end of audience participation on dance-band nemos for* Monitor! *(28)*

Some of *Monitor's* band remotes took place on New Year's Eve as part of a tradition that NBC Radio had begun decades earlier. Since at least 1929, the network had broadcast band performances across the nation as New Year's arrived in each time zone. Originally called *Pursuing Time Across the Country,* the New Year's Eve remotes were, in *Monitor's* years, known more simply as *NBC's All-Star Parade of Bands.* Gene Garnes Sr. engineered some of them:

The broadcast team as it always was consisted of myself and the announcer, period. There was always a radio line pre-installed by the phone company and either an intercom or phone line so I could speak to Radio City's transmission depart-ment for testing and getting accurate time to set our watches. NBC's portable equipment had a four-microphone capability, so we generally did a remote pick-up with a maximum of four mics. Since the engineer worked alone until the announcer showed up (about 20 minutes before show time), the engineer could only carry so much. We relied on taxi service to get us to our destinations so four mics, a half-dozen cables, a telephone, a program headset an amplifier/mixer were about all a guy could handle. (29) We never had a rehearsal for any of these, and sometimes we hit the air and the announcer was simply not close enough to the mic. Even killing all the other mics wouldn't do the job—just too much orchestra coming through the announce mic. Our headphones were the cheapest money could buy—the company's attitude was that the headset you misplaced was something no one would steal, anyway, and it was within budget, as well. Then you must remember we were sitting on stage with the band most times, and if you think the engineer could really hear what he was doing, think some more. (30)

Other "remotes" were actually recorded earlier on tape. Garnes recalls a series of them that worked extraordinarily well, possibly because he used his own equipment, not NBC's, to get them:

I had amassed some state-of-the-art tape recording equip-ment. When given an especially worthy assignment, I would use my own equipment, which was generally superior to that of the company in those days. At that time, management pol-icy was if RCA didn't make it, NBC didn't use it! One of the VP's in charge of Monitor knew of my interest in pipe organs and would ask that I be assigned to record Christmas carols with Dick Leibert at the Radio City Music Hall on an annual basis. After the initial mono effort around 1960, I used my own equipment and subsequently taped (other) shows in stereo. Count Basie with vocalist Joe Williams was an especially rewarding effort. That tape was nothing short of spectacular. It was split up into a series of 10-minute vignettes and aired over one weekend on Monitor. *(31)*

Some of *Monitor's* remotes didn't originate very far from Radio Central—in fact, they originated just outside the studio. For years, NBC brought tourists through the studio area during *Monitor* broadcasts.

Very often we would have the host go out (from the glass-enclosed studio) with the remote microphone and have a conversation with the tour (members). Ask where they came from. It worked very well. Those days, you didn't worry about someone from the tour making obscene comments. And people could go home and say, "I was on NBC last week." (32)

Most of the time, the technical aspects of the program went smoothly. When they didn't—when a live remote failed, or a tape running a feature story broke—comedians Bob and Ray were there, live, at Radio Central to "cover" for the fluff until *Monitor* producers could decide where to go next. Dave Garroway recalled one major "glitch" that not even Bob and Ray could help fix:

I recall one exotic night when at 7:01 all the lights went off (at Radio Central). We went on the air at 7, and at 7:01 all the illumination went off. The pilot lights on the switchboard didn't go off, but you can't see much by those. And we had scripts, you know, to read, and commercials to read, and for several minutes it was really black. No one smoked, you see,

and then somebody found some matches, and there was one or
two in the pack, just one or two.
Meanwhile, screaming and yelling for flashlights—no flash-
lights. And the matches burned for a few seconds, went out,
and it was all black again.
And then somebody got a flashlight, and then, by that, we could
read on one microphone. And it took 20 minutes to get two or
three flashlights, and the lights went on at that time. (33)

And then there were the mistakes that were man-made:

There was a small booth containing one microphone feeding
the Monitor *control room and it was primarily used only for*
network identification. There would be an announcer
assigned there, and his job was to say, "This is the NBC Radio
Network," and then the Monitor *engineer would ring*
chimes. This would occur, on average, every half hour.
(An announcer) was on duty in the booth, waiting to give the net-
work ID, and one of the engineers was having a discussion with
him from the doorway of the booth. This required (the announcer)
to turn away from the mic and the "On Air" indicator.
The conversation ended, unbeknownst to (the announcer) just
as the "On Air" light went on, and he responded to the other
conversationalist by saying, "You do, and I'll cut your balls
off. This is the NBC Radio Network." (34)

On *Monitor's* 10th birthday in June 1965, Radio Central became the
hub of a giant on-air celebration. Steve White, who was then in charge of
special features for the show, devised a gimmick that lasted the entire
weekend. He invited Academy Award-winning lyricist Sammy Cahn and
his partner, Jimmy Van Heusen, to stay in Radio Central on Saturday and
Sunday to write a *Monitor* birthday song.

Monitor's hosts frequently talked with Cahn and Van Heusen throughout the weekend to see how the job was coming. Finally, on the Sunday night *Monitor* segment, the task was accomplished, and singer Steve Lawrence went to Radio Central. Accompanied by several NBC musicians, he sang the birthday song as the anniversary program came to an end. (35)

By that 10th anniversary, *Monitor* had been on the air over 11,000 hours—far more than any other radio show in history. The program had aired more than 60,000 remote broadcasts, presented more than 75,000 interviews and played more than 150,000 songs. It had revolutionized, and breathed new life into, network radio.

> Monitor *capitalized on its own formlessness, allowing its subject matter at all times to determine the amount of program time allotted to it. On a continuous basis throughout the weekend,* Monitor *provided listeners with an ear to the world—something the television networks were not equipped to do. (36)*

John Chancellor said that *Monitor,* besides being entertaining, performed a valuable public service:

> *It did tie up the whole country. It made you feel that you were a citizen of the United States, not just a Chicagoan or a New Yorker listening to a radio station.*
> *For most of all of those weekends, you did have a feeling that the country was sharing and participating in a single enterprise, and that was magic. (37)*

Years after he created *Monitor,* Pat Weaver summed up the program's appeal this way:

> *If you were an adult citizen in the country, you would miss a great deal if you missed* Monitor, *because the major things that were happening would be touched on, covered, and you'd*

*be there, and you'd hear the man who said it from the place he
said it. And if it were a cultural event, you'd hear a few bars
of whatever it was, and you would be there. (38)*

Taking listeners "there" was something *Monitor* did quite well, indeed,
for most of its broadcast life. On the air, the program succeeded in making
it all seem so effortless.

It wasn't.

6

The Weekly Scramble

Getting *Monitor* on the air each weekend required the intense efforts of dozens of people working hundreds of hours during the week in a mad dash against the clock.

Preparation for the Saturday and Sunday broadcasts started on Monday morning. Generally, that's when those most responsible for generating the ideas, finding the people and setting up the interviews and remotes for the following weekend's broadcasts would meet with *Monitor's* executive producer. In the first few months *Monitor* was on the air, the EP was Jim Fleming. He left before the end of '55 and was replaced briefly by Frank Papp, who in turn was succeeded by Al Capstaff.

Capstaff, who also had been a *Monitor* communicator, held the EP job for several years and was succeeded by Marx Loeb. After a short time, Loeb turned over the reins to Bob Maurer, who became *Monitor's* longest-tenured executive producer. Maurer held the job from 1962 until late '73.

Burroughs (Buck) Prince had the key job of assignment editor for years. It was his responsibility to find the news and feature stories, present them as possible *Monitor* features to the executive producer and then, when approval came, turn the ideas into actual on-air pieces. Other important players who worked on story ideas over the years included feature news editor Fitzgerald Smith and features editor Constance (Capi) Petrash.

Their professional lives were pressure-packed—on their shoulders fell the burden of filling an immense amount of broadcast time each weekend.

Just how tough was it to fill 40 hours (or 32, in 1956, or 16, in 1961) of programming a week? Extremely. As *Monitor's* format changed over the years, the program relied less and less on affiliate-station "stringers" who could send in feature material that would be aired and, in the process, fill up some of that time. Increasingly as the years wore on, the burden of "filling" *Monitor* each weekend was shifted to NBC staff members and news correspondents—and to the program hosts themselves, who were asked to do more and more taped interviews with celebrities, authors and others.

During the '60s and early '70s, Maurer was the man on the hottest seat for *Monitor.* He ultimately was responsible for every news or feature story that went on the air. *Monitor's* music was handled by another NBC executive, Bob Wogan—so Maurer could concentrate on the program's editorial content.

Each Monday, *Monitor's* news and feature editors would meet with Maurer in his office, "and I'd talk over what they had to offer, what personalities were available, what authors were available, what other things were available. And then I would decide." (1)

In other words, Maurer would determine, to a great extent, how *Monitor* would sound during most of the '60s and into the '70s. It was his choice about which big-name stars would be interviewed—and which wouldn't—and which authors would appear—and which wouldn't. He decided, to a great extent, the program's format.

After Maurer made his decisions, the news and feature editors started the process of making the appropriate contacts to set up the interviews or reports needed for the following weekend. At this point, on Monday, *Monitor's* production teams—the people responsible for putting the material on the air—were not at work because they had been on duty the previous Saturday or Sunday with their programs.

Thus, Tuesday became the first day that any of the teams would come back to the office—in this case, it would be the teams that had shepherded

Saturday's *Monitor* segments. Their days off had been Sunday and Monday, and now they were ready to start their end of the production process.

In the '60s, when *Monitor* had been reduced to the 16-hour broadcast schedule it would keep for much of the rest of its life, each three-hour *Monitor* segment (and the four-hour segment on Sunday afternoon) had its own separate production team, composed of a producer-director, a writer and an assistant producer. Each person on that team had his or her own specific set of duties that did not overlap another team member's.

The producer-director was ultimately in charge of the nuts-and-bolts production of his particular segment. That included editing tapes and coordinating all material into his three (or four) hour block. During the week, that individual would be on hand for the interviews his segment host did—and then edit them into broadcast form. On show day, the producer-director would be in the control room with several technical people and be the ultimate arbiter of what went out from Studio 5B, the glass-enclosed announce studio where *Monitor's* hosts worked.

A writer was in charge of preparing all scripts and introductions to taped features. The producer gave the writer the finished, edited reports so the writer could properly script introductions and "tag" lines for the program host. On broadcast day, the writer was responsible for changing scripts to reflect breaking news events.

A production assistant was in charge of the music for each segment. During the broadcast, that assistant would handle all music tapes and records and cue the turntable engineer about when to play them.

In effect, *Monitor* was five separate programs under the same umbrella title. Each of the individual production teams operated independently of the others, though they generally knew what was in the other segments. In the mid-60s, the Saturday morning segment's team included producer Bill Malcolm, writer Bill O'Connell and production assistant Carole Wendt. Saturday afternoon's team included producer George Voutsas, writer Dick Petrow and PA Bonnie Buchanan. On Saturday night *Monitor,* the team was producer Parker Gibbs, writer Charlie Garment and PA Shirley Robinson.

The production team for Sunday afternoon *Monitor* was composed of producer Fred Weihe, writer Catherine Faulconer and PA Jean Houston. Sunday night *Monitor* featured the team of producer Bud Drake, writer Dick Bruner and PA Melissa Blanton. (2)

It was these team members who would meet with Maurer each week to receive their marching orders.

"We were told that this week you'd have such-and-such a guest and this many 'Ring Around the World' segments," remembers long-time *Monitor* writer Charles Garment. "If we had any ideas of our own, we could bring that up. We'd say, 'Maybe you ought to get such-and-such a musician or singer or comedian or movie star.'" (3)

Monitor producer-director Bud Drake remembers many meetings he and other team members had with Maurer during the week before each broadcast. Drake says the executive producer was always looking for new ideas and recalls a frequent scenario: "Maurer would have fits. 'You mean we've got 25 creative, intelligent people, and there isn't a single idea here?' And nobody would open their mouths." (4)

Garment remembers that the meetings generally went smoothly:

> *When we came into the meeting, they'd say, "This is what you're going to have." And we could place it (within the body of the program) ourselves. For example, if you had actors and authors, producers could place the people (wherever they wanted) in the hours."*
>
> *There weren't strict rules that you had to have this or that. (5)*

Once the discussions were over, Drake and the other producers went to work, putting the individual pieces of the *Monitor* program puzzle together for their segments. They would often call the segment host to find out when he (or, occasionally, she) was available to interview the author or the famous star who would appear on the air in a few days.

During the '60s, Monitor's hosts tended to be people who were heavily involved in TV or movies, so scheduling them for interviews was no small task. "I would never make a commitment (to a guest) unless the host was available," remembers Drake. (6)

Once the interview was done, the producer spent hour after hour in an edit booth, picking just the right questions and answers to fit into a three or four-minute package. Once that package was completed, it went to Maurer for approval: "The final edited version would come to me, and I would listen to it and either approve it or make suggestions." (7)

Sometimes that system didn't keep mistakes from making it on the air:

> One afternoon (Bud Drake and I) were working on an espe-
> cially difficult tape from the Vietnam War. One of our corre-
> spondents sent the tape in, and it was an interview with some
> official. In the background you could hear ambiance created
> by some of the troops in the vicinity.
> We finished the tape to Bud's satisfaction, and that was the
> end of it until it was broadcast. I don't remember what I was
> doing when it aired, but I happened to be by a speaker and
> thought I'd just pay attention to see how my editing efforts
> sounded from within the show.
> Halfway through the piece, I ignored the primary content to
> concentrate on the background voices. And there was, as clear
> as you could imagine, the word "motherf——er."
> I couldn't believe my ears. How could we both have missed
> this during the editing? The next week I told Bud about what
> I had heard, and he brought the tape with him to the editing
> room, and we both listened, this time to the background, and
> there it was.
> He didn't say much, and I suppose held his breath to wait for
> any reaction from listeners or management. There was none!
> We both got away with that one! (8)

While producers were working on the taped material that would air in their broadcasts, the writers stayed busy. Garment says that on Tuesday or Wednesday, depending on when he started his workweek,

> *I would start to get material together—random stuff, bits and pieces, oddball stories that might have come up in the news, to fit in certain areas. Not shocking. We weren't allowed to be shocking. The first day was sort of haphazard. I got some material and would write some stuff that day. I spent (the first day) doing bits and pieces. (9)*

Often, the writers got to do the interviews that would air the following weekend. The process was called a "stop-tape," or "stop-start" interview. The writer's questions would be edited out, leaving only the guest's answers. Then, when the interview was broadcast, the program host read the questions that the writer had asked:

> *The host would be live, and he would say, "Now my guest is Gregory Peck, and it's a delight to have you here, Mr. Peck." The engineer would hit a button, and Peck would give his answer (on tape). We had the end-cue on the script, at which point the cart (tape playback machine) would stop, and the host would then ask another question, live.*
> *If it's done correctly, there's no way you can tell that Peck wasn't in the studio. (10)*

And listeners never knew the guest, in this case Mr. Peck, had never spoken to the *Monitor* host who asked the questions on the air, but instead had been interviewed by a writer who worked in virtual anonymity on the broadcast.

And in an age where broadcasting was still pretty much a man's world, many of those writers, over the years, were women. "We had a goodly number of women writers on the show," Garment says. "This is way back before women seemed to get an equal shake, but in our show, they were there." (11)

As the workweek progressed, segment production assistants (many of whom were also women) were working to get the music together for the three-hour broadcast they were assigned to. Melissa Blanton worked as a PA on *Monitor* in 1966:

> *We had certain records we were to play. You had to do a certain number of required records and then you could choose the rest of your records. I always tried to get a Bobby Darin record in. Everybody knew I loved him, and as luck would have it, the week he came to* Monitor *to be interviewed, I was on vacation. (12)*

In addition, the production assistants would make a rough rundown, or "routine sheet," of each half-hour of the three-hour segment, based on decisions made by the producer and writer, who decided in which order which elements world play. How many elements could be used in each half-hour, how long the musical cuts could be and how short or long the writing would be changed with each *Monitor* half-hour. A typical page from a routine sheet looked like this one, from Saturday morning *Monitor* on July 21, 1973 (courtesy of Gene Garnes Jr.)

```
Bud Drake              MONITOR ROUTINE SHEET              Page 1
Charles                                                   July 21, 1973
Garment
Melanie Turner         HOST: BILL CULLEN                  9:00:00 AM
9:00:00      BEEPER
             BILL:     OPEN
             CART:     RCIA COMMERCIAL              (1:00)
             CART:     RAID COMMERCIAL              (0:30)
             BEEPER
9:05:30      DISC/BILL: PICK YOURSELF UP
                       ENOCH LIGHT                  ENDS
                       RUNS 3:00
                       PLAY TOP & FADE ON CUE

9:07:40      BEEPER
9:07:45      CART:     THEME# 5F                    (0:11)
FADE
9:07:55      BILL      B B                          AT :11
                                                    (0:25)
9:08:20      DISC/BILL: BOOGIE WOOGIE BUGLE BOY
                       (2:17) ENDS
                       BETTE MIDLER
                       RUNS 2:17 ID OVER :15 SNEAK
9:10:40      TAPE:     JOE GARAGIOLA                (3:52)
                       (INCLUDES 1:00 RALLY WAX & :30
                       ZEREX)
9:14:35      BILL:     BEACON CUE                   (0:05)
             BEEPER                                 (1:10)
9:14:40      CART:     "D"—CUT # 1
```

Monitor's format changed over the years, but in the mid-60s, it went something like this: During the first 30-minute period of each hour, *Monitor* began after *News on the Hour* ended. For most of *Monitor's* run, *NOTH* aired for five and one-half minutes. Then, stations received a two-minute music "fill" before *Monitor* began at seven-minutes and 40-seconds after the hour (the Beacon took up from five to 10 seconds). Stations got a one-minute cutaway for local commercials within that *Monitor* segment—and another 30 seconds at 29:30 after the hour for a local commercial. (In *Monitor's* early years, stations received more local cutaways during certain parts of the broadcast day.)

Throw in the program's own commercial minutes—ranging up to five or more each half-hour on Saturday mornings to much lesser amounts during the other four weekend segments—and that's how much time each producer and writer and production assistant had to "fill."

The problem was that on Wednesday or Thursday, the various interviews and other recorded elements weren't finished—so production assistants had to "guess" how long they'd have for music and choose back-up selections in case an interview that was planned for three minutes just couldn't be cut any shorter than three and a half or even four minutes.

As soon as a producer finished editing a piece and received approval from Maurer, the segment writer would get it so that he or she could listen and craft an appropriate introduction that somehow tied in with the material about to be heard.

In other words, "scripts would not be started from the top" of each three-hour segment, according to Garment. "Bits and pieces were written first, perhaps some entertaining factoids." (13)

Producers left it to the writers to make the script material "flow" from one segment element to another. Garment and Drake worked closely together for years on a variety of *Monitor* segments and developed an unspoken feel for what each other wanted. "Charlie was so damn good," recalls Drake. "He just had an instinct for writing to time." (14)

That made the production process a whole lot easier for both of them, since Drake could concentrate on producing the reports without worrying about how they would be "tied together" on the air, and Garment could concentrate on writing without worrying about whether program elements would be there on time.

Crunch time came Friday. Drake remembers that as his busiest night when he was producing Gene Rayburn's Saturday morning *Monitor* segment. He would often work late into the evening to finish editing the pieces that would air in just a few hours the following morning.

Garment recalls Thursdays and Fridays as his busiest days. He knew that Maurer liked to have the scripts done early on Fridays so the EP could read them and make changes if needed.

But Garment says he was a "last-minute writer," meaning he often wouldn't begin scripting the "top of the program" (the first few minutes of each *Monitor* half-hour) until Thursday afternoon or Friday morning. The pressure was intense.

> *I used to have terrible nightmares of trying to get scripts ready for Saturday for the show, and I had dreams where I never quite got it done on time. I can't describe how horrific it was in the dream. (15)*

Once the scripts were done, Maurer read every page: "All the scripts would come to me and I would go through them and see if everything was as I thought it should be." He gave writers freedom because, he says, "You have to respect their ability." The executive producer did not take any scripts home. (16)

Once final approval came from Maurer, multiple copies of the scripts would be made and distributed to the various *Monitor* staffers who needed them: the producer-director, the writer, the production assistant, the engineers who would put all of *Monitor's* sounds on the air within a few hours—and, of course, a copy for the program's host.

On broadcast day, each segment's production team would show up at Radio Central well before airtime.

> *We would get to the studio, make sure all the tapes were in place, all the cassettes or cartridges, and then go in and chat with whoever the host was. "Hi, Gene, how you doing, what's happening, how's Helen (Rayburn's wife), what'd you do last night, see a play, movie, okay." (17)*

Generally, the *Monitor* host arrived about a half-hour before airtime to read over the scripts. The writer or producer would be sure to point out any peculiarities involving any of the show's elements:

Gene, we're going to do this to begin with, and in case you haven't heard the tape, he's going to say so-and-so. So when you say this up front, you're referring to what he'll say. And when you come to the end, you're reacting to this. (18)

As airtime approached, the control room filled up. The producer-director was there, along with the writer, the production assistant, a control-board engineer, and another engineer for the turntables. Other engineers were in nearby playback rooms, ready to load the cart-tapes or reel-to-reel tapes that would air. *Monitor's* host in Studio 5B was separated from the control room by soundproof glass.

Each hour began with *Monitor News on the Hour*, which had been produced independently from the *Monitor* program itself. Separate writers and editors put together each newscast. Both the newscast and the *Monitor* broadcast were engineered from the same control room—but the newscaster read his copy in an announce booth next to Studio 5B, where the *Monitor* host sat (or stood, in Gene Rayburn's case—he often announced his entire three-hour segment while standing).

Sometimes, the newscaster was a tad farther away from the *Monitor* host—those times when the newscast originated from NBC's Washington, D.C., studios. The introduction would still be done by the *Monitor* host in New York's Studio 5B, followed by the toss to the newsperson in Washington.

It was a complex production setup. The newscast began with *Monitor's* host, in 5B, introducing it: "*NBC Monitor News on the Hour*, brought to you by (sponsor). Now, here is (name of newscaster)."

The newscaster read for a few minutes and then "broke" for a commercial. The *Monitor* host then re-introduced him by saying, "Once again, (name of newscaster)." More reading from the newscaster, another commercial, one last bit of news, then a sign-off by the *Monitor* host ("Listen again on the hour when (sponsor) brings you *NBC Monitor News*"), and *Monitor* was ready to begin.

The first order of business: two minutes of music "fill" that affiliates could either air or replace with their local commercials. Then, the Beacon—often played off a disk—signaled the start of something big— *Monitor*—followed by the program's theme-of-the-moment.

In the control room, the producer-director cued the program host as the engineer opened the host's microphone. It was lightning fast—and hosts knew not to speak until they'd been cued because their words would never make it on the air.

The host would read the appropriate introduction (probably to a musical selection), and the turntable engineer—who had been handed the record moments before by the production assistant—would spin it on cue from the producer-director or the assistant. The host's microphone would be clicked shut (astute listeners could hear that "click" if they knew what to listen for), and *Monitor* was off and running.

Keeping the show on time was the job of the production assistant. If a host ad-libbed too much, something would have to be dropped—never a commercial, of course, but often "fill" script pages about quirky items that had been written to add humor or pacing to the broadcast. The producer-director was the one who would make the decision about what to drop.

The time clock was harsh: Near the half-hour mark, *Monitor* needed to be off the air (with the chimes having been sounded) by 29:30. The production assistant made sure that the turntable engineer started the half-hour's last musical selection (generally an instrumental) on an exact-time basis so that it would end at the appropriate time.

At the exact half-hour mark, the host would speak again to introduce five minutes of *Monitor* music that local stations could either put on their air or "cover" with local newscasts and commercials. (This five-minute optional cutaway, providing plenty of time for local-station commercials, was another of Pat Weaver's brilliant ideas to induce stations to air *Monitor*. He provided a similar cutaway window on his *Today Show* on NBC-TV, and that feature exists to this day.)

At 35 after the hour, the Beacon played again, signaling stations to return to the network. Another *Monitor* theme aired, and the production process began again. This time, the imperative was to be off the air by 58:50, giving stations one-minute-10 seconds for commercials and a station identification.

Bud Drake remembers those three-hour segments as "constant tension." He also remembers standing up the entire time in the control room with his head "right in the speaker so I could hear very nuance" of what went out on the air. (19)

Then, at the top of the next hour, the Beacon signaled the start of another newscast. The script for it had been brought in just moments earlier by the newscast's anchor or producer. After the *Monitor* host introduced the news and the switch was made to the announce booth where the newscaster was reading, a few of the production team members would head to Studio 5B to talk with the host and "let down our hair and relax for five minutes." (20)

Then it was back to the control room to begin another *Monitor* segment.

What happened when a breaking news story intruded on a carefully scripted *Monitor* hour? The segment producer would make the decision about how to handle it and then turn it over to the writer to get it done. Garment remembers that many times he had to "get the stuff edited in a hurry, write a quick introduction and then run with the damn thing, tape goes to the engineer, copy or scripts to the director and producer and man on the air." And, if the story was big enough, "You just dumped everything else." (21)

And what happened at the end of each team's three-hour broadcast (four, on Sunday afternoons)? When their program ended, team members didn't stick around to talk about how well—or poorly—things had gone. "Everybody ran for the hills," Garment says. "We always felt the show was alive and didn't need an autopsy." (22)

There would be time enough for post-mortems when the various production teams came back to work the following Tuesday or Wednesday. But not *that* much time.

Another *Monitor* weekend was on the way—another 16 hours had to be filled—and it was time to get jumping again.

7

Big-Name Hosts

Dave Garroway and Wolfman Jack. Bill Cullen and Murray the K. Gene Rayburn and Don "Imus in the Morning."

Ask almost anyone today about what those TV and radio personalities had in common, and you'll likely get a blank stare.

But Garroway and Wolfman and Cullen and Murray and Rayburn and Imus and dozens of others over two decades shared at least one professional achievement:

They all hosted *Monitor*.

Garroway—the quirky, low-key, master ad-libber—was the best-known of the early emcees. He had been hosting the *Today Show* on NBC-TV for three years when he made his debut on *Monitor*.

Garroway—whose first reaction was to say "no" when he was asked to host *Monitor*—played a prominent role on the first broadcast on June 12, 1955, and then stayed around through the end of the 1950s and into the '60s.

He settled comfortably into the Sunday night *Monitor* slot, sometimes appearing on air from 8 to 10 p.m. and other times from 7 to 10 p.m. His forte was the personal interview with big-name stars who would gladly make their way to Radio Central to appear on radio's biggest network show with one of TV's brightest stars.

There is no doubt that Garroway's presence during *Monitor's* early years was vitally important to the program's acceptance by critics, listeners and advertisers. With Garroway on board, *Monitor* took on the instant appearance of importance. And the fact that Garroway hosted *Monitor* on Sunday nights and then appeared on *Today* on television during the week gave the radio program an immeasurable amount of prestige.

As important as Garroway was, he had a downside for some staffers—behavior that at times bordered on the rude and arrogant and at others seemed simply baffling.

Longtime writer Charles Garment remembers the first time he ever worked with Garroway on *Monitor*. Garment had put together a considerable amount of written material for the star, who arrived late for his air shift, right in the middle of *News on the Hour*. Thus, Garroway had no time to pre-read Garment's script.

> *And he sat down and he picked up the script and he started ad-libbing something which was total gibberish. It had no connection with the spot he was introducing. And then he hammered his way through the next 15 or 20 minutes. I was livid. Now I'm not a man who puts up with anything. I don't work that way. So I'm sitting there (next to the studio) and Parker (Gibbs, the segment producer) knows how mad I am, and he brings Garroway in, and I looked at him. And Parker says, "Dave, this is Charlie Garment." And Garroway said, "I'm sorry I sort of messed up your script there."*
> *And I said, "Well, if you had come in on time and looked at it, you'd probably have done a better job. But it's your show, and if you want to (expletive) it up, it's up to you." And Parker turned white. And Garroway stood there with his mouth open. There was a big silence, and then he said, "I'm going to try to do better the rest of the night." And he read every word beautifully. (1)*

Garment also recalls another Sunday night *Monitor* segment in which Garroway insisted that staffers "put up a screen, one of those folding screens, so that he wouldn't be seen by too many people" who might be walking outside Radio Central's glass-enclosed studio. "He wanted privacy. They put (the screen) up in the studio, somewhere around the (announcers') table. He was a weird man." (2)

Garroway also could be dismissive of others. Producer Bud Drake says he worked with Garroway for several weeks. The first night, "I walked into the studio, and he was talking to an announcer. I waited, then said, 'Dave, I'm Bud Drake.' He looked at me and said, 'So you are,' and continued his conversation. That's the kind of (man) he was." (3)

Garroway stayed on *Monitor* until early 1961. By that time, he was winding down his career on *Today*, and NBC decided he would have to leave the radio program as well. For all his eccentricities, and occasional strange behavior, Garroway's loss was major in terms of the star power he took with him.

Years later, Garroway returned to *Monitor*—as a guest, not a host—on the program's last broadcast in 1975. John Bartholomew Tucker asked him what he remembered about the program's first broadcast, on which Garroway played a big part:

GARROWAY: Not the slightest. Fact, to be honest, really, I have fewer recollections of *Monitor* than I have of getting off and on the elevator out there. *Monitor* was very much linear. We came in, we did little bits and pieces, and there were several of us spread out. Pete Roberts sat next to me for years, and only once in awhile something in the control room would go wrong, would we look up from our *Argosy* magazine or whatever we were studying that week.
TUCKER: Did you ever play any kind of practical jokes on each other, you and Peter Roberts and any of the other fellows?
GARROWAY: We seldom spoke to each other (LAUGHTER FROM THE CONTROL ROOM) Pete Roberts and I were on all the time, but we had our little duties. We had to check off this and check off that, and we were busy with the routine and then whatever we were reading. We talked more outside than we did inside. (4)

Years later, another *Monitor* host, Monty Hall, would recall that he worked with Garroway twice on his Sunday night show and that "he never said a word to me during the three hours that we were together." (5)

Frank Blair, who was Garroway's newsreader on the *Today Show*, also had a long and successful career on *Monitor*. Blair became the program's first Saturday morning host, working from 8 a.m until noon, along with a variety of co-hosts, including long-time announcers Frank Gallop and Don Russell. He also hosted Sunday night *Monitor* for several years in the 1960s and occasionally contributed special reports to the program at other times.

Blair remembered that "we had a lot of laughs on *Monitor*. Things would go wrong occasionally, and it gave us the opportunity to get back to the good old days of radio when you could ad-lib and use your own brain for a change." (6) It was, he said, "amazing how fast the time would fly (on *Monitor*) because we always had something to do, and something interesting to do." (7)

In the early years of the show, Hugh Downs followed Blair as host, or "communicator," each Saturday at noon. After his success on Pat Weaver's midday *Home* program on NBC-TV, Downs says he was delighted when Weaver asked him to host *Monitor*—delighted, and nerve-wracked:

> *I had been on the network before, but really not on a big deal. In Chicago, I occasionally did a five-minute newscast that went to maybe 80 stations. My network experience was pretty limited as far as any real visibility or importance went. So when I came to* Monitor, *it was a very big deal, I thought. I was very nervous about the first shift I did. (8)*

Downs would arrive for his shift at least an hour early to look over the script. And while much of what he said on the air had been written by others, including questions for the guests who made their way to the studio for interviews, he prided himself on being able to ad-lib inquiries whenever the interviewee's answer opened up new avenues for questioning.

Because of Downs' ability to speak extemporaneously, his frequent co-communicator on *Monitor*, Peter Roberts, often called him "Professor Downs"—"not on the air so much, but when I'd come in, he'd always say, 'Professor Downs.'" (9)

Downs remained on *Monitor* as a co-host for several years, finally leaving when the pressures of doing a nightly TV Show (*Tonight* with Jack Paar) conflicted with his weekend duties on radio. However, he would come back frequently as a contributor of special features, most often interviewing media celebrities about their hobbies, families or homes.

Downs loved *Monitor*—and loves telling the story that Ted Koppel, the longtime host of ABC-TV's *Nightline*, related to him: "When I was doing *Monitor*, (Koppel) was an NBC guide. And he remembers bringing groups of people to look through the glass (at Radio Central) at me, doing *Monitor*. Isn't that amazing?" (10)

Monty Hall is best known as the long-time host of one of television's most successful game shows, *Let's Make A Deal*. But before *Deal* debuted, Hall spent many Saturday nights at Radio Central as a *Monitor* host from 8 until midnight. He recalls that he would arrive at 7 and look over the agenda to familiarize himself with the rundown of events coming up on his segment. He said there was very little script to look at and that he ad-libbed his way into many of the features.

During most of Hall's *Monitor* career, he was paired with renowned NBC newsman and commentator Morgan Beatty. The two were on the air on a memorable Saturday night that Hall recalls to this day:

> *I remember that we were going to go to Ottawa, Canada, for a live interview between Prince Philip, Queen Elizabeth and (NBC newsman) Merrill Mueller. I screamingly protested to (producer) Murray Burnett that the Queen does not do interviews ad-lib and especially not from a phone booth! When, of course, the interview never happened and NBC had egg on its*

> *face (I told Murray again and again that it wouldn't), he did-*
> *n't speak to me for two weeks. (11)*

Charles Garment was *Monitor's* writer that night and remembers the situation exactly as Hall describes. He says sometime Saturday afternoon, Mueller called *Monitor,* and producer Burnett got the idea that the Queen would speak to the program on the phone, possibly from a telephone booth. Burnett made the decision to promote this potential interview on the air frequently.

> *And Monty was saying, "This can't be. There's no way the*
> *Queen is going to speak to us on the phone, especially a public*
> *phone. Forget it. It's not true."*
> *And Murray wouldn't listen. He was foaming at the mouth*
> *with excitement. He loved this whole idea. So he had Morgan*
> *(Beatty, the co-host) say the promos. We kept promoting this*
> *thing and promoting this thing. (12)*

What followed, according to Garment, was one of the funniest scenes in *Monitor* history. When it became apparent that the Queen was not going to make a call from a phone booth to Radio Central, Garment wrote a script in which Beatty would introduce Jinx Falkenberg, an NBC personality who was in Ottawa with Mueller. At a certain point, soon after Falkenberg began speaking, the *Monitor* engineer would purposely cut her off so that Beatty, back at Radio Central, could then apologize to the audience for the "line failure" that made it impossible to get the Queen on the air.

In other words, Beatty would pretend the show had technical problems, and the audience would never know the difference. It didn't work.

> *Morgan does the introduction. They cut Jinx off, and Morgan*
> *was supposed to say, "Jinx, are you there, Jinx?" And Morgan*
> *read it, I can't quite describe it. He did it almost like a little*
> *rhyme with a lot of rhythm to it, and it just sounded so*
> *absolutely ridiculous, I remember I fell on the floor in the control*

*room. Everybody else in the control room was hysterical. I've
never seen so many people dying from over-laughing. The whole
thing was so preposterous.*

*And Monty was saying, "I told you so. I told you so." Monty
insisted, right through the whole thing, "You will not get the
Queen on. I will not be part of this." (13)*

That particular disastrous night aside, Hall remembers *Monitor* fondly:
"This is what live radio is all about. It (*Monitor*) should be carried by some
network today instead of the endless hours of talk-talk-talk—most of it
angry nonsense." (14)

Another of the early *Monitor* "communicators" was veteran NBC Radio
announcer Ben Grauer. He had spent years announcing Arturo Toscanini's
NBC Symphony broadcasts and many other network shows. By the time
Monitor debuted, Grauer had 25 years of network radio experience.

His voice was the first one listeners heard on *Monitor's* initial broadcast
in 1955, but it wasn't until September of that year that he was made a regular host. As he joked years later, "It took me three months to tell them
what a great mistake (NBC made) in not having me." Grauer enjoyed
working on *Monitor*—though, like Garroway, he had doubts about
whether it could work:

*I was so indoctrinated and hardened into the idea of 15-minute
or half-hour shows, it was like, this will never change, this is the
establishment. And very shrewdly, NBC realized they had to make
some new adaptation to the waning power of radio vis-a-vis television, so they evolved this magazine idea which was* Monitor.
*And I didn't understand it at first. How could a thing like that
work? Well, it worked superbly and I was glad to be part of it.*
Monitor *was a delight because it was fresh and new. (15)*

Grauer often was paired with veteran network announcer Frank Gallop,
whose style suggested a certain dignified and suave manner. Grauer made a

point of kidding Gallop on the air in order to get him to "loosen up." One such incident nearly proved to be disastrous:

> *Once I walked out of the studio for a moment. I came back in and Frank was sitting in front of the mic. And some music was playing. I thought we were off the air. I said, "Here you are, Frank, you——." And he looked at me, and his eyes bulged out a quarter of an inch and came back. Luckily, he was on the air, about to make an announcement, but he hadn't started it, and the music covered what I said. (16)*

Grauer recalled that writers prepared scripts for Gallop and himself, "But we didn't chat their way. We did our own chatter. We just went off the script like mad."

Another man who often ignored the script became *Monitor's* longest-tenured—and perhaps most-beloved—host. Gene Rayburn first appeared on *Monitor* in the early 1960s. By then, the original idea of two co-hosts had gone by the wayside, and each *Monitor* segment was now solo-anchored. Rayburn—and the other hosts—were freer to take liberties with the scripts without worrying about putting their co-host in the position of having to respond when, perhaps, they were not prepared to do so.

And Rayburn was extraordinarily well-qualified to ad-lib his way around a broadcast. He had spent years doing so—first, as a mainstay on WNEW Radio in New York, where he teamed up with Jack Lescoulie and later with Dee Finch on a morning show that some say created the drive-time formula still in use at stations around the nation. Rayburn and his partners played records and ad-libbed about anything that interested them.

Rayburn left WNEW to join NBC Radio in 1952, where he had another early-morning program. He also became Steve Allen's announcer on the first *Tonight Show* on NBC-TV, where he read the news and appeared in many of the skits along with comedians like Louis Nye and Buddy Hackett.

In addition, Rayburn hosted TV game shows such as *Play Your Hunch* and *Tic Tac Dough*. But his biggest TV success—the one for which he would be forever known—started in 1962, when he was chosen as host for *The Match Game* on NBC-TV.

That game show would become one of network TV's longest-lasting and most successful. It aired on NBC until 1969 and then on CBS from 1973 to 1979. During the CBS years, it was often TV's top-rated game show. Rayburn received five Daytime Emmy nominations for his hosting skills.

Gene instantly became a success when he started on *Monitor* in the early 1960s. In the early years, he often hosted Saturday afternoon or evening *Monitor*, but by the mid-60s he was firmly ensconced as the Saturday morning host, where he would remain until the early '70s. For millions of Americans, listening to Gene Rayburn on Saturday morning *Monitor* became a tradition.

And as the years passed, that Saturday morning segment became *Monitor's* most important. The 9 a.m. to noon slot that Rayburn hosted became—and remained—the most heavily sponsored part of *Monitor*. Advertisers were well aware that millions of Americans "hit the road" on Saturday mornings—for weekend outings, trips to the store or to friends' homes—and those sponsors tended to purchase air time on that *Monitor* segment more than on any other.

Rayburn's sassy, irreverent, "I'm going to be naughty" type of presentation seemed perfect for the time period. He brought energy and enthusiasm to Saturday mornings. "He had the right kind of sound for that time of day," says Garment, who was Rayburn's Saturday morning writer for years. "He gave a great ride to whatever I wrote. He was also a personable and friendly guy." (17)

Bud Drake, who produced many of Rayburn's Saturday morning shows, goes farther: "Rayburn was a great guy. He was very popular with everyone in the building. He was very adaptable and very directable and very easy to work with." (18)

Drake and Garment agree on something else: Gene Rayburn loved to ad-lib, and that occasionally could spell trouble. "You just had to watch him all the time," says Drake.

One memorable ad-lib came in 1967, when Rayburn was doing a live commercial for Ace Combs. Midway through the 60-second commercial, Gene veered from the script, which had just mentioned Ace's "unbreakable" quality compared with "no-name" combs:

> *RAYBURN: Let me just see what kind of comb I've got. I got a no-name comb in my pocket! No wonder it was scratching my scalp. I'll break it. Matter of fact (LAUGHING) it won't break! Now this is one of those cheap, no-break combs here. Anyway, for the finest comb you can buy, deal yourself an Ace...(19)*

Rayburn's ad-libs were often inspired. During the opening of one of his programs in 1969, he did a take-off on a weekend story "theme" that was running through all the *Monitor* segments—physical fitness.

> *(RAYBURN PUFFING) Hello there. Gene Rayburn here. And if my voice sounds a little weird, it's because I'm jogging as I talk with you. (SOUND OF RAYBURN JOGGING IN PLACE) I'm jogging because* Monitor *has dedicated this weekend to physical fitness and beauty, and we'll be discussing this with (MORE JOGGING) experts and celebrities and (PUFFING) I've got to take a break now. So, while I jog over to the couch, you listen to the newest from the Peppermint Rainbow, "Don't Love Me Unless It's Forever" (VOICE TRAILS OFF AS IF HE IS JOGGING AWAY) (20)*

Rayburn's extensive radio and TV experience made it easy for him to "fill" whatever amount of time was needed, in the event a scheduled event did not occur, or something else went wrong on *Monitor.* Production assistant Melissa Blanton remembers one particular incident:

We had a Bert Kampfert song, and we started it, backtimed.
And (producer) Parker Gibbs said, "That record is too fast.
It's on the wrong speed." We realized he was right, and we
were going to come out of it 30 or 60 seconds ahead.
Parker just said to Gene, "We're going to come out early.
Stretch." And Rayburn did it. He was wonderful. Of course, I
was feeling devastated, because I hadn't noticed the thing was
on the wrong speed. (21)

By the mid-60s, many of *Monitor's* celebrity interviews were on tape.
The program's hosts, and the guests, would be brought together at Radio
Central during the week to record the piece that would air the following
Saturday or Sunday. One of those taping sessions involved Rayburn and
actor Walter Matthau, who was there to talk about his most recent movie.
Drake was the producer.

Rayburn said, "Boy, that's a pretty spiffy suit you've got on."
And Matthau said, "Well, it's from the costume department."
And Rayburn said, "You mean that?"
Matthau said, "Yes, when you do a movie, you get to keep the
wardrobe. It's been cut for you and built for you." So Matthau
took off the jacket, and the band said something like Warner
Brothers or whatever.
And so he turned and said, "Everything, from my underwear
on out." And with that Matthau drops his pants.
Meanwhile, the tours are going by, right outside Radio
Central, and there's Walter Matthau standing there, with his
pants down around his ankles, showing Rayburn the label on
the back of his shorts. (22)

Rayburn was part of one of the biggest fiascos in *Monitor* history. Fans
of the program have been passing around tapes of it for years. On the
tape, NBC newsman Dean Mell is heard finishing up a *News on the Hour*

segment, followed by someone clearly stating the word, "bullsh—."
Rayburn—sounding flustered—is heard next: "Ring (pause)—Listen
again on the hour when Ford with 50 new models for 1970 brings you
NBC Monitor News."

The explanation most often heard about that unfortunate moment is
that Rayburn and a staffer were having an argument when Rayburn's mic
was opened. According to writer Charlie Garment, that story is wrong—
and he should know. He's the one who uttered the "B" word.

In a telephone interview, he set the record straight about what really
happened in Radio Central that day in 1969. During *News on the Hour,*
Garment and producer Parker Gibbs went into the studio to chat with
Rayburn during the five minutes in which the news would come from a
next-door announce booth:

> *I was having an argument with Parker. Gene was sitting at the*
> *microphone. I was standing in the studio. Parker was sitting on a*
> *couch in the studio. I had my back to the control room. We were*
> *having an argument about Vietnam, and Parker said something*
> *that was totally outrageous to me, and I said, "Bullsh—."*
> *I didn't know they had opened Gene's mic just before I uttered*
> *the magic word. And Gene went almost into shock. I know he*
> *stumbled and mumbled and said whatever he said to get out*
> *of there. And everybody turned and looked at me, and we*
> *looked at each other, and I said, "That got out." And they*
> *said, "That got out." (23)*

Garment says that within two minutes, a program executive called him
from home to discuss the unfortunate word. Several NBC affiliates were
said to have received calls about the matter, and one affiliate sent Garment
a roll of toilet paper.

Garment kept his job, and to this day the tape of his indiscretion continues to be recycled among *Monitor* enthusiasts.

Monitor staffers appreciated Rayburn's charm and easy-going manner. So did his fans—even if they didn't know exactly who he was. Gene Garnes Sr., who helped engineer *Monitor* for many years, remembers a trip he and Rayburn made to Chicago for a *Monitor* promotion:

> *My wife, myself and Gene were riding the same elevator to our (hotel) lobby and upon exiting, we walked leisurely down the concourse. A lady thought she recognized Gene and approached him, saying, "Mr. Ames, may I have your autograph, please?" Gene responded cordially, took the lady's pen and paper, wrote a brief generic message and signed it, "Ed Ames." After the fan was beyond earshot, Mr. Rayburn revealed to us that this happened frequently and he preferred not to embarrass the fan but (instead) make the fan's day.*
>
> *He also mentioned that in a past discussion with Ed Ames (a well-known singer of the time), it was revealed that he, too, had been mistaken for Gene on occasion. (24)*

Gene Rayburn became *Monitor's* mainstay—remaining as Saturday morning host while every other program segment underwent numerous hosting changes. Rayburn stayed on *Monitor* more than nine years—and when he finally left the program in 1973, it signified the end of an era not just for *Monitor*, but for millions of his Saturday morning fans who had made listening to his irreverent, often unpredictable, comments "must-hear" radio for years.

During Rayburn's long tenure on *Monitor*, many other hosts came and went. Bert Parks was one—he began as Saturday afternoon host in 1961 and remained with the program, off and on, for most of the '60s. Parks was, at the time, best-known for hosting the *Miss America* pageant on television, but he also had an extensive radio career. In fact, back in the late '40s his *Stop the Music* network radio program had single-handedly destroyed comedian Fred Allen's competing radio program on NBC.

Parks handled *Monitor's* hosting chores with ease, rarely departing from his script and rarely missing a word or beat.

Another TV pro, Hal March, took over the Sunday afternoon *Monitor* slot in 1961. March was well-known as the former emcee of TV's *$64,000 Question* game show. One of that program's early winners was a young psychologist named Dr. Joyce Brothers, who parlayed her knowledge of boxing into the top prize. Years later, Brothers would also show up on *Monitor*.

Ed Bryce, one of the pioneers of early TV, also took a turn as a substitute Sunday afternoon host in the early '60s. Bryce had played Captain Strong in *Tom Corbett, Space Cadet*—one of TV's earliest space adventures—and had a 14-year career on *The Guiding Light* soap opera on TV

Another *Monitor* host in the early '60s was Wayne Howell, a night-time disk jockey on WNBC Radio in New York—and *Monitor's* Saturday night host for a time. The busy Howell also served as an announcer on many TV game shows, including *Concentration, Name That Tune* and *Meet Your Match*.

Several veteran stars of movies, radio and television showed up as *Monitor* hosts in the '60s. Jim Backus was one of them. Today, hardly anyone remembers that Backus had a distinguished movie career, including a role as James Dean's father in *Rebel Without a Cause*.

Instead, he is remembered for two things—as Thurston Howell III on TV's *Gilligan's Island* and the voice of the cartoon character Mr. Magoo. Yes, Backus occasionally did the Magoo voice on *Monitor*.

Before Gene Rayburn took over the Saturday morning *Monitor* slot—and kept it for many years—David Wayne was Saturday morning's host. Wayne had a long stage and screen career and later would star in TV's *Ellery Queen*.

The *Monitor* staff liked working with Wayne—he was easy-going, liked to get out of his chair and dance while the music was playing, and always wanted to have a good time: "When they switched us off, and they'd go to news and things like that, then we'd start bandying some of our brand of humor about, and it was fun, really fun. I enjoyed that program enormously."

For a time, Wayne had trouble reading the scripts, so the crew got him a typewriter with bigger typeface. Wayne remembered it differently: "I think the writers needed to see their material better." And he recalled one particular goof he made on the air: "I lost my place one time. I started re-reading a page I'd already read. We eventually got back on the track. Maybe the material was so important I felt it had to be read twice." (25)

Another famous stage, movie and TV star who hosted *Monitor* in the mid-60s was James Daly. Like David Wayne, Daly was well-liked by the *Monitor* staff, who gave him an unofficial "good host award" because he was never late, read through his whole script ahead of time and rehearsed if necessary.

So what was this well-prepared host's worst mistake on the air? He mis-read his own name. "An old announcer who'd been in the business for years rushed out of the booth and grabbed me and said, 'Welcome to the club. You mispronounced your own name'"

Daly remembered *Monitor* fondly: "Nice job, I remember lots of fun, lots of laughter." (26) James Daly also was one of *Monitor's* few hosts who left on his own, preferring to devote more time to television.

Stage and movie star Barry Nelson also charmed *Monitor's* audience as a host. During much of the time he appeared on *Monitor,* he was starring in *Cactus Flower* on Broadway.

> *I had a lot of fun at* Monitor, *mostly, I think, interviewing people. It gave me a chance to meet a lot of people I wouldn't ordinarily have met, to talk with them and have those five-ten minute interviews. It took up my Sundays, but it kept me out of trouble. (27)*

Nelson hosted Sunday afternoon *Monitor* for several years. Melissa Blanton remembers that he treated *Monitor* staffers well: "One Easter Sunday, he came in and brought candy for the women on his crew. He was extremely thoughtful." (28)

Nelson's successor on Sunday afternoons was no stranger to the program. Indeed, Henry Morgan had been one of the original participants on *Monitor's* very first broadcast in 1955, giving reviews of television programs. Invariably, those reviews were satirical, and often they were scathing—a pattern Henry had developed in the late 1930s and '40s with his nightly program on Mutual Radio.

After his first year or so on *Monitor,* Morgan's appearances became infrequent—until the mid-60s, when he came back first as a Saturday night host and then settled into the Sunday afternoon slot for the rest of the decade.

Earlier in his career, Henry made a name for himself by commenting about people in the news, the weather, or his sponsors. On *Monitor,* he toned down the types of attacks against advertisers that had made him famous—but he was always ready to deviate from the script if the mood struck him.

And it often struck him. Once, in giving a *Monitor* tip for drivers, Morgan said, "If you have trouble keeping your windshield from fogging up, check into some of the products on the market for solving that problem. There's a spray; there's a cloth treated with a chemical. Also you could tell your wife to cut down on the hot air." (29)

During another *Monitor* tip, this one about proper dinner etiquette, Morgan ad- libbed liberally:

> *If you're having a dinner party, and you have someone doing the serving, (LAUGHS) I don't know anybody who can afford that. But if you can, the hostess is no longer served first. That's an old custom which originated in the dangerous days of the Borgias. It was intended to reassure guests that the food was not poisoned. In other words, if the hostess fell off her chair, you didn't eat. Well, unless you think your guests think you're trying to poison them, serve the guest of honor, or the lady seated to the right of*

the host, first. And then eat while it's hot. This is Emily Morgan. (30)

Another time, giving a tip for Christmas shopping, Morgan's ad-lib was reminiscent of the ones he did on his old radio show:

Now a tip, by George. For Christmas. You know it's too late even now to do your shopping early. So do it late. Do it Christmas Eve. Most of the big department stores are deserted. Shopping is quick, it's easy, and the sales people despise you. And, of course, they won't have much stock left. But then you're a little out of your mind, anyway, to go shopping on Christmas Eve (LAUGHS). (31)

And yet another Morgan tip on *Monitor* went this way:

A Monitor tip for motorists. A windshield rubbed with sliced onion will stay clear on rainy days. And if you rub it on the wrong side, your friends will stay clear, too. (32)

Morgan began one *Monitor* segment during the 1969 Christmas holiday season by commenting on the hordes of holiday shoppers who had descended on Manhattan:

Morgan here, high above the crowds in New York City. What I'd like to know is, if everybody from out of town comes into New York after Thanksgiving, which they have done today, who's home eating all that leftover turkey? A panel of judges will consider the answer and the winner will receive a wishbone. (33)

On that same broadcast, Morgan had a tip for Christmas gift-givers:

If you have to wrap something odd-shaped, like a lump of coal (PAUSE AND SIGH). They could hire somebody to do this. Well, they did.

So if you have to (LAUGHS) wrap something odd-shaped like a lump of coal, don't try to do it with regular wrapping paper. Use aluminum firl (SIC) because it'll cling to the irregular shape and that'll make a nice funny-looking package. But why me?

Now this from the Three M Company. If you're going to give a Christmas gift to someone very—this is much more intelligent than what I just said—if you're going to give a Christmas gift to someone very small in years... (34)

And yet another holiday tip, courtesy of "Santa" Morgan on *Monitor:*

Listen, this Christmas, when you put up your tree, set it in a pan of water. Add a half a cup of sugar to the water. It may do something good to help the tree last longer, but it will certainly be a holiday treat for the ants in your house. (35)

A week later, Henry started his broadcast by saying:

Morgan for Monitor. *May I spell that for you? It's M-O-R-G-A-N. I want you to remember the spelling because I finally thought of something you can get me for Christmas. It's described as 86-proof chess. Giant chessmen, each of which holds a fifth of a special distillation of a certain spirituous drink and a four-foot square rug to play the game on. Or to fall down on, if you're (LAUGHS) a real loser and you drink the chessmen. That's H-E-N-R-Y M-O-R-G-A-N. (36)*

Morgan always had a high opinion of himself, and that occasionally—according to at least one person who worked with him—made him difficult to work with. Bud Drake produced several of Morgan's *Monitor* segments:

> *One night we were on the air, and a tape was coming up, and I got on the talkback and said, "Henry, this lady wants to be known as…"*
> *He exploded. "Don't you tell me how to pronounce it. I am probably the most experienced name pronouncer in the business!" I was so angry. I dashed into the studio and said, "Who do you think I'm trying to make look good, you or me?" He said, "Aw, get out of here." Finally the tape came up. And he used a phony accent as introduction. (37)*

This self-styled "most experienced pronouncer" delighted in purposely mispronouncing words or names he found absurd. One of them belonged to a pop singer of the '60s named Englebert Humperdink. Once, after Humperdink's *Winter World of Love* aired on *Monitor*, Morgan followed up this way: "There is a good thing about the name Humperdink. If you were lined up alphabetically, you'd be about in the middle." (38)

Another time, he called the singer "Englestam Hunkerdank."

And another time, following a *Monitor* piece in which the reporter had pronounced the word, "ACC-li-ma-ted," Morgan immediately corrected him by saying it was pronounced "acc-CLI-ma-ted."

That was Henry Morgan. Opinionated. Brash. Sometimes off-the-wall. Some people didn't like it his act, but his fans—and there were many of them—adored it.

He was *Monitor's* man on Sunday afternoons from the mid-60s until 1970. His replacement was also brash, opinionated and off-the-wall.

Ted Brown was no satirist. But the WNEW and WNBC Radio disk jockey could be a wild man at times on the air—ad-libbing outrageous remarks, breaking into a foreign accent, and occasionally driving *Monitor* producers crazy because his ravings would put the broadcasts well behind-time.

He often would introduce himself on air by saying: "Ladies and gentle-men, it is I, Ted Brown, here, 4-6, dark hair, green, piercing eyes, cat-like movements…"

At any point while his microphone was on, Brown would, and could, deviate from his script to get a laugh:

BROWN: Let's talk about you. Have you ever thought about going on a vacation to Tunisia, hum? You haven't been out of the bathroom in three weeks. (LAUGHTER) Now listen to me. We've got a place for you, oh, I tell you. Those little ad-libs I throw in. As my mother once said:
WOMAN: My son, the announcer.
BROWN: Yes, then again, three out of four women I meet say:
WOMAN: Oh, Mr. Brown, would you mind shutting up and playing the record?
BROWN: I will, I will. (39)

On one broadcast, the script called for Brown to introduce a report by Graham Kerr, the so-called Galloping Gourmet. Brown read the introduc-tion in a voice that sounded as if it belonged to a mobster:

BROWN: Uh, I wanted to ask you something. You know, if you're a good cook, you see, and you feed your husband well, he'll love you. If you don't, uh, he ain't gonna be too happy when he comes home, and he'll come busting through the door and say:
VOICE OF SCREAMING MAN: Where are you, you old bat?
BROWN (now in English aristocratic accent) So I suggest you listen to Graham Kerr and he'll tell you so much about cooking that your husband will come home and say, "I love you, let me count the ways." Ha, ha, ha, ha. I don't think you'll even have time to cook.

What followed was a Kerr report about how snails consummate the sex act, including word that it takes five seconds for the actual act and two and one-half hours to get into position. Afterward, Brown commented:

*And actually, I don't know what he's getting so excited about.
I never thought there was any other way. I mean, you know,
that's rather quick, if you want to know. I mean, it should
take approximately two and a half hours. (CLEARS
THROAT, LAUGHS) What's the matter with that guy? Is he
crazy or something (NOISE OF CROWD MUMBLING).
He shouldn't talk about things like that, you know? You know
how many snails right now are very embarrassed about this
whole thing? Snails who listen to* Monitor? *We've got a big
audience in snails, by the way. In the Southwest, we're
Number One with snails. (40)*

Brown often made fun of, or pretended to be critical of, *Monitor* correspondents. During one introduction to a movie review by Gene Shalit,
Brown gave the critic a "warning":

*Now, my opinion is, it's a great movie, but that's my opinion.
(BROWN SOUNDING LIKE A MOBSTER) Gene Shalit,
you give it to Jules Feiffer in the back, baby, and I'm gonna
give it to you. (41)*

Shalit liked the movie—and *Monitor* fans liked Brown so well that he
stayed on the Sunday afternoon program until 1972.

His successor was the man who made TV's *Jeopardy* famous. No, it's
not the person you think.

Jeopardy's original host—and to this day, the one many consider the
program's best—was Art Fleming. He had started his career in radio, so it
was no stretch for him to host *Monitor*. His tenure on Sunday afternoons
was much shorter than Morgan's or Brown's, and by 1973 Sunday afternoon *Monitor* was hosted by New York radio personality Dan Daniel.

During a good part of the '60s, Saturday afternoon *Monitor* became
synonymous with one man—Ed McMahon. Johnny Carson's legendary

second banana on *The Tonight Show* had always wanted to do radio and had been a fan of *Monitor's* for years:

> *I built a pool house when I lived in Philadelphia, and I used to get up on the top of my pool house (to) put the roof on. I had a little transistor radio with me, and I used to listen to* Monitor. *I always found* Monitor *to be great radio.*

One of the on-air quirks he was noted for was giving the temperature in Tegucigalpa. In general, though, Ed stuck to the scripts and delivered them in a smooth, professional way. That was tougher than it seemed to listeners, because as the years wore on, McMahon had loosened up on his rehearsal style:

> *(*Monitor*) became a hanging-out grounds for all my pals. On a Saturday afternoon I was in there for three, three-and-a-half hours, and my buddies in the business, they'd kind of congregate in that big Central Control where we do* Monitor. *And it became a thing where we'd be in a gab-fest, and be telling a joke or telling a story, and you'd get the click from the control room, the warning that you were up live any second. And it was amazing how right in the middle of a story, you could say, "So these two girls got off a streetcar—this is* Monitor. *" I remember that toward the end, it was like almost like dancing on fire—how close you could stop talking and be on the air and be in total control, have your faculties and be running. (42)*

One of McMahon's buddies who showed up one day in 1967 at Radio Central was his *Tonight Show* boss, Johnny Carson. It was a weekday, and Carson was taping an interview that would air on McMahon's Saturday afternoon segment. Bud Drake was there to produce the piece, which turned out to one of *Monitor's* funniest interviews:

(Carson) came in and did the interview in a little booth. Finally at the end of it, Ed says, "Well, thank you very much, John." And John says, "What do you mean, 'Thank you very much'? That's the end of it? I gave up a whole day to do this." And Ed says, "Well, I'm sorry, but 'Monitor Goes Fishing' is next." And of course Johnny had a lot of fun. (43)

McMahon enjoyed being on *Monitor*. He occasionally would mention the program during banter with Carson on *Tonight*—and at least once, Carson "complained" that he, McMahon, had many outside activities, including *Monitor,* while the host himself had nothing else in his life.

During Carson's early years on *Tonight*, the TV program originated from New York and occasionally went West a few times each year. During those visits, McMahon could not appear on *Monitor*—but often, following *Tonight's* last Friday evening in California, he took a red-eye flight back to New York so that he could be on the air at 3 p.m. with *Monitor* the next day.

It was the *Tonight Show's* permanent move to California that ended McMahon's tenure on *Monitor*. Ed asked NBC if he could originate his *Monitor* segment from California, but the production logistics were too tough.

In order to keep Ed's voice on the air in some manner, *Monitor* created a niche for him—doing celebrity interviews. So even though McMahon no longer ruled Saturday afternoons, his voice could occasionally still be heard. His departure as host left a void for his *Monitor* fans—and for his segment's production assistants in the control room. Melissa Blanton says that at the halfway point of McMahon's three-hour *Monitor* segment—at 4:30 p.m.—the host would go into the control room "and rub the production assistant's neck. It felt good." (44)

McMahon's successor on *Monitor* came from left field—or, more precisely, from the catcher's position. Joe Garagiola was a retired major-league ballplayer who was making his living as a sports announcer. He was quick-witted, funny—and never hesitated to joke about his modest lifetime stats.

Garagiola had been doing two or three-minute *Monitor* sports features for years before he became the permanent Saturday afternoon host in the late-60s. He was popular because he was not a classic "announcer" with deep, mellifluous tones. He came across as a "regular guy" whom you'd enjoy spending a Saturday with, talking baseball and enjoying your favorite beverage.

And that on-air impression, says Bud Drake, was exactly the way Joe was off-the-air: "He was just a doll. He was just so funny and such a congenial, great guy. I loved him. He and I got along very well." (45)

Joe hosted Saturday afternoon's segment for only a couple of years, but he contributed more than 2500 sports commentaries to *Monitor* over many years. He often was irreverent and funny. Once, he discussed plans (that never came to fruition) for the United States to convert to the metric system and how that could impact sports:

> *How far is the distance from home plate to first base? Well, for a guy in a slump, it could seem like four miles and all uphill. Actually, the rulebook says it's 90 feet, but it may not say that for too much longer…*
> *Should the distance from base to base be 27 meters? That would make the distance shorter than it is now. 28 meters would be longer. The third choice would be that home plate to first base would measure 27.4320 meters. I bet the groundskeepers would love that. You'd need a college degree to lay down a foul line.*
> *Would I care to make a prediction? I'll tell you something. That's one I wouldn't touch with a three-meter pole. (46)*

Joe could deliver a funny punch line, but he also could be serious when it was needed. He was on the air the Saturday afternoon in June 1968 when assassinated Senator Robert Kennedy's body was being taken by train to Arlington National Cemetery. Garagiola's somber, measured delivery that afternoon under difficult circumstances was a model for all broadcasters—and this, from someone without a news background or significant professional media training.

Joe Garagiola was an original.

So was the man who followed him as Saturday afternoon *Monitor* host. Not only was Bill Cullen an original, he was in the process of becoming a king—the king of television game shows.

Cullen had an extensive radio career—including several years as host of the morning show on NBC's New York radio station. But he made his biggest mark as the man who hosted more TV game shows than any other person. He is perhaps most famous for originating *The Price is Right*—that's right, HE hosted that program—but his credits list many others. He also was a regular panelist for years on the *I've Got a Secret* television program.

Bill Cullen brought a low-key, self-effacing presentation style to *Monitor*. Unlike Ted Brown, for example, Cullen rarely made fun of other performers. Most often, if he ad-libbed during the program, it was to make an ironic comment comparing himself (usually in an unfavorable light) to the person just heard on the air.

Once, for example, after hearing a report from *Monitor's* resident psychologist, Dr. Joyce Brothers, who had urged a female letter-writer to, in effect, give her husband more sex, Cullen followed up this way.

> *I got a problem too, at home. I got a problem there. A personal problem. I guess I shouldn't discuss it. I won't discuss it because my wife would cut me off without a cent. (LAUGHS) Thank you, Doctor. Doctor Brothers welcomes letters from* Monitor *listeners. You may address her (LAUGHS) in care of NBC* Monitor, *30 Rockefeller Plaza, New York.*
>
> *Here's a new release—let's change the subject—by Peggy Lee.*

Sometimes he would simply put himself down, albeit in a gentle manner. One example: "Welcome again to the Big M, where we have a lot going for you. This is Bill Cullen, an exception to the foregoing."

And another example, this time during a promo Cullen read for the upcoming Sunday night *Monitor* program:

> *On the lighter side, some tips from the* Garden Encyclopedia, *on how to make your gardening easier and more rewarding. You know, I have a brown thumb. Maybe I should listen. Or if not that, at least, wash my hands. Anyway, all joking aside, not necessarily, plan to join host Jim Lowe later. (47)*

Cullen did a variety of things for *Monitor*. He hosted the Saturday afternoon segment for a time; he often sat in for other hosts; and he voiced many special features for the program. The king of TV game shows made for pleasant listening on many of *Monitor's* weekends.

Saturday night *Monitor* had a variety of hosts in the '60s, including Gene Rayburn (until he moved to his "permanent" slot on Saturday mornings), Henry Morgan (until HE moved to Sundays) and Ted Steele (who stayed for several years).

And then came Murray Kaufman. That was his real name, but on the air, he was simply "Murray the K." He had become New York's hottest disk jockey in the early '60s with the help of a wide variety of stunts, including broadcasting his show from the streets, subways and practically anywhere else that would have him.

During the Beatles' American invasion in the early '60s, Murray jumped on the very big bandwagon he had seen coming and became, in effect, the Beatles' foremost promoter. He tried to—and succeeded in—associating himself so closely with the Fab Four that you would have been forgiven if you'd thought he was on their payroll. He broadcast from their hotel room, co-hosted their performance at Carnegie Hall and later went to England with them to emcee a performance at Wembley Stadium.

He became known, unofficially, as "the Fifth Beatle."

But by the late-60s, Murray's act had worn down a bit. His hiring by *Monitor* was a risk—could he keep himself under control on the air and not alienate those NBC affiliates for whom a rock-and-roll presentation would be an instant turn-off?

The answer was, surprisingly to many, yes. On *Monitor,* Murray the K was pleasant and low-key. If the occasion arose, he would ad-lib from his vast musical knowledge base or perhaps hint about things he knew about a certain performer—but generally he followed the script the way it was written.

After he'd been on *Monitor* awhile, he even joked that "they said it would never work." It did work—for several years. No screaming. No yelling. Just Murray the K, introducing features and music and signing off his Saturday night shows with "Ciao, and love." The Fifth Beatle had, indeed, proven the skeptics wrong. He had made it work.

After Murray left Saturday night *Monitor,* several people hosted that segment. One of them was a woman—Cindy Adams, who would later go on to become one of America's most famous newspaper columnists. Cindy's forte then, on *Monitor,* as well as later, in print, was the celebrity interview.

One of Saturday night *Monitor*'s hosts was a secret right up until the moment he spoke on air. All day one Saturday in December 1972, *Monitor* promoted a surprise "guest host" for that evening's show, which would begin after the 7 p.m. *News on the Hour.*

At 7:05 p.m.—when, normally, the program host would introduce a couple of minutes of music "fill" (local stations could insert their commercials there, if they chose), whose voice should be heard but—Gene Rayburn's:

> *Hi, there, this is Gene Rayburn. (CHUCKLES) No, I'm not mixed up. I know I'm not your Saturday night host on* Monitor. *I've done my stint. But there's a surprise coming up for you, because your host for the evening is—ah, I can't tell you. It wouldn't be a surprise if I told you. Stick around and find out who it is.*

Meantime, Bob Mitchell plays Where or When. *That's not the question. "Who" is the question.*

The music played, followed by the *Monitor* Beacon, signifying the start of the program. Then, after the theme, the voice heard next was—NOT the guest host's:

> *This is* Monitor, *and this is Ed McMahon, with a very special assignment. I'm about to introduce the host of this segment, and it's a real pleasure for me. Welcome to* Monitor, *Mr. Frank Sinatra Junior.*

What followed were several minutes of McMahon interviewing the young Sinatra, who said he could remember when *Monitor* started:

> *I can remember when NBC weekend radio was just NBC weekend radio; and I can recall, I believe if I'm not mistaken, it was about 1955, or so, when they first put it (*Monitor*) together. I can recall being in California and hearing the duh-duh-dee, duh-duh-dee, duh-duh-dee, coming across the radio, and I said, "Now, I wonder what that noise is." (48)*

Then Sinatra turned the tables and interviewed McMahon, asking him how he became Carson's second banana on *The Tonight Show.*

The interview ended with McMahon instructing Sinatra on how to give the station cutaway cue, which was "You're on the *Monitor* Beacon." Sinatra thus began a three-week guest hosting stint on Saturday night *Monitor.* During each of those weeks, he performed live at the Rainbow Grill on top of the RCA Building from 9:30 to 10 p.m.—and *Monitor* carried those performances live.

In contrast to Saturday night *Monitor,* the Sunday night version had relatively few hosts during the program's entire 20-year run. Garroway had been the emcee for six years; he was succeeded by Frank McGee, the NBC newsman who brought a serious demeanor to the program and who urged producers to make it newsier. They did, and for a time, during the early '60s, *Monitor* on Sunday nights was, essentially, a three-hour news summary of the week's events.

It was a critical hit—winning a Peabody Award and bringing a considerable amount of praise for the effort.

McGee stayed on *Monitor* until mid-1964, when he was succeeded by Frank Blair, who was making his second run at hosting the show. Blair, of course, had been one of the program's first communicators, handling the Saturday morning segment during much of the '50s.

Blair's was also a serious approach, befitting the style of the *Today Show* newsreader that he was. Following Blair came Brad Crandall, a New York talk-show host in the days when talk shows were just getting their feet off the ground in radio.

And then came Jim Lowe. Actually, Lowe had been hanging around *Monitor* for years—he'd hosted the Saturday night segment from 1962 until '64, before succeeding Crandall as Sunday night host in 1969. Lowe would become the Sunday night fixture until late '73—and his combined years on *Monitor* would be exceeded only by Gene Rayburn's.

Lowe was born in Springfield, Missouri—graduated from the University of Missouri—and wanted to be in radio virtually all his life. His move up the broadcasting ladder was fast—he went from Missouri to Indianapolis and then on to NBC's Chicago radio station.

There, he got to work with his idol, Dave Garroway. For years, he had listened to Garroway at night, as WMAQ's powerful signal boomed his *1160 Club* program across the Midwest. "It was the most brilliant local radio show that I've ever heard in my life. He was so articulate."(49) Garroway became the biggest influence in Lowe's professional life.

Garroway went to New York in 1952 to host TV's *Today Show*. Lowe arrived in New York two years later—not to do radio, but records. On his way to radio stardom, Lowe took a temporary detour by recording a hit song, *Green Door*, that became one of the big pop tunes of the mid-50s.

But music was "really just a side career that sort of got out of hand. My main thrust was always radio." (50)

The record helped get him the job he really wanted—as an on-air host at WCBS Radio. Then in 1959, WNBC hired Lowe as a disk jockey, and three years later he turned up on Saturday night *Monitor* as host. It was a dream come true because he had wanted to host it for years: "*Monitor* was brilliant. I heard it driving around up in New England, the first weekend of *Monitor.* I thought, 'What a wonderful concept, to go all weekend long.'" (51)

Lowe's first stint on *Monitor* was brief. He left WNBC in 1964 to work at WNEW in New York, and his *Monitor* job disappeared. Five years later, WNBC hired him back, and there he was again on *Monitor*, this time on the shift he would keep for several years—Sunday nights from 7 to 10 p.m. He would arrive at the studio 45 minutes early to look over the scripts:

> *I really didn't do much preparation. I went through my life being on the radio four hours a day, in Chicago and New York, on local radio. And people said, "How do you prepare for this four hours?" And I said, "Well the only thing I can tell you is, my whole life is a preparation." (52)*

Lowe delighted in finding parts of the script that he could embellish, and the producers let him do it: "I had grown up ad-libbing, and they knew that, and so they knew that I could do that. And I think maybe they gave me a little more leeway than the other anchors would have had." (53)

One of the proudest moments of his life, he says, involved an ad-lib that he made on a Sunday night in December 1971 after NBC's legendary chief David Sarnoff died. Lowe and Ben Grauer hosted a *Monitor* special:

> *For many years, we had only said (on the air), "This is the NBC Radio Network," which I always thought cheapened the network. So at the end of this hour, with no permission at all, with seven or eight people in the control room, I just boomed*

> *it. I said, "This is the National Broadcasting Company,"*
> *which hadn't been said in years.*
> *In the control room, they all threw their arms into the air. But*
> *I went for it, because this was the thing I'd grown up with."*
> *(54)*

In keeping with his low-key, almost intimate on-air approach, Lowe's "signature" phrase on *Monitor*—the one that, to this day, he is most known for—involved his listeners. He'd often refer them as "old friend," as in, "Stay on the line, old friend."

Jim Lowe did—he stayed on the *Monitor* Beacon almost until the Beacon faded. He calls his tenure "seven of the happiest years of my life in radio."

By the time Lowe left *Monitor* in late 1973, the list of people who had, at one time or another, emceed the program was a long one. Mel Allen (who hosted Saturday morning *Monitor* for a couple of years), Al "Jazzbo" Collins, Tony Randall (one producer said he never quite got the hang of the format), Garry Moore, Durward Kirby, Bill Hayes, Bob Haymes, Art Ford, the husband and wife team of Jerry Stiller and Anne Meara, Mel Brandt, Gene Hamilton, even soon-to-be TV news superstar David Brinkley, were some of the "others" who took their turns in front of *Monitor's* mics at Radio Central.

They all had the advantage of hosting the program before the times of desperation set in. By 1973, things were changing on *Monitor*—and new, different hosts would be brought on board to announce a different kind of *Monitor*.

It would have the same name—but it would not be the *Monitor* that most listeners would fondly remember years later.

8

"Miss Monitor"

So who WAS that stunning redhead with the sexy voice who gave weather forecasts on *Monitor* in a way that had never been done before, anytime or anywhere?

She was a small-town girl from Georgia who grew up knowing exactly what she wanted to do with her life—paint pictures.

But a funny thing happened to Tedi Thurman on her way to becoming an artist. She took a couple of momentous detours that eventually led her to Radio Central and the job that made hers one of the most famous voices in the world.

Tedi was born in Midville, Georgia, just outside Augusta. Her father was president and chief executive officer of a local bank and also owned an automobile agency. She was the youngest of four children—her sister was the oldest, followed by two brothers.

She attended Midville schools and remembers that from a very early age she wanted to become an artist. "I used to draw cartoons and thought I wanted to do that," she says. "Then I thought I wanted to learn to paint." (1)

Tedi saw a few fashion magazines when she was growing up, but mostly her mother "subscribed to things like *Good Housekeeping* and *Ladies Home Journal.* I saw more of those than anything else." And, yes, she listened to radio—but never thought about working in it.

After high school, Tedi enrolled in the University of Georgia in Athens but decided she didn't like college life. She attended the High Museum's art school in Atlanta for a time, where she studied her first love—painting—and then moved to Washington, D.C., to take more art classes.

She spent a year in the nation's capital and was good enough to win an award for her artwork. But fate—or luck—had already interceded in her life. During her time in D.C., she was constantly in demand as the subject of other artists' works. "People were always painting me, telling me I should become a model."

That idea had never occurred to her, but once it did, she jumped at it. Through the friend of a friend, Tedi was introduced to a modeling agent. One thing led to another, and suddenly Tedi Thurman found herself in New York—"I wasn't scared, I was excited"—and on the cover of *Vogue* magazine. It was her first job.

The next few years found Tedi on the cover of virtually every major fashion magazine—so many that she can't count them—and in numerous newspaper ads. That exposure brought her to the attention of TV producers, who cast her in several bit parts on the live dramas that were so much a staple of the "Golden Age of TV" in the early to mid-1950s.

And because, by that time, she loved New York City so much, she turned down the chance to go into movies. She received several contract offers from major Hollywood studios—including one that would have allowed her "right on the spot" to star in a film. "I didn't take it. I was so busy as a model. I preferred living in New York. I didn't want to go to California. That was a very bad decision, of course."

But Tedi was about to make up for that. As a result of her TV appearances, she had been noticed by one of the people hired to put on a new type of radio program. That program, of course, was *Monitor*—and Mike Zeamer would become one of its first writers and producers. He asked Tedi if she would consider doing the weather on *Monitor*. She was intrigued.

"It was undiscovered land, and it sounded interesting, something to pursue." So Tedi began showing up at the RCA Building to do a series of audition tapes for the upcoming broadcast. "The more I did over there, the more interesting it got, and the more exciting it got. I could see it was going to be big."

NBC signed her to an exclusive contract, which effectively ended her modeling career. She gave up the glamorous life of being a magazine "cover girl" to become, in mid-1955, and forever, "Miss Monitor."

Starting that first Sunday on the air, June 12, Tedi would appear, live, on *Monitor* frequently throughout the weekend and deliver the forecasts in a way that *New York Times* critic Jack Gould described as "an irresistible invitation to an unforgettable evening." (2) She was on-air so often during those early weekends that program creator Pat Weaver "called into the producers and said, 'She's sounding tired. You'd better let her go home.'" Thereafter, "Miss Monitor" was scheduled in blocks of time, with a hour or two in between appearances so she could rest.

From the start, "Miss Monitor" was designed to be sexy. Tedi had a naturally low voice, and, at the suggestion of *Monitor's* producers, "I sort of softened it and made it go with the music. I intentionally put more emphasis on the sex angle." It worked.

Tedi's style, backed by a lush musical score, made the temperatures sound considerably hotter than they appear on the printed page: "In Atlanta, the temperature is 59, fair. Cleveland, 34, snow. Boston, 41, cloudy. Phoenix, 62, fair. New York City, 43, partly cloudy. Paris, 38, cloudy. New Orleans, 48, rain. Albuquerque, 67, fair. Chicago, 32, cloudy."

No matter how many forecasts she did during a *Monitor* weekend, and no matter how many cities she mentioned, Tedi always started with Atlanta because she had attended art school there. She wrote and produced her own weather forecasts. "I had to get them myself, from the U.S. Weather Bureau in Washington." Frequently on Saturday and Sunday, she called the bureau and asked for the forecasts. "Sometimes I would pick the cities as topicals, according to what was going on, of interest (on

Monitor)." Other times, she would pick cities simply on the basis of what interested her at the moment. She had complete freedom to choose any cities she wanted.

In the early days of *Monitor,* Tedi would arrive at Radio Central either right at the program's 8 a.m. Saturday start or just a bit later. She was given an announce booth next to Radio Central's massive glass-enclosed studio that housed the communicators. It was from that booth that she would make her telephone calls to the weather bureau and go on the air with her forecasts.

She generally would appear on *Monitor* every hour, or half-hour, depending on the program's needs. Occasionally, she was called on to fill time, much as Bob and Ray would do, if a scheduled live remote failed to come up. She always prepared more than enough script material for her minute or two-minute segments, just "in case they needed to stretch out the time."

Tedi's weather forecasts generally came off without a hitch—with one memorable exception. It was the time Henry Morgan set her script on fire.

"I don't know why they put him in my booth. He wasn't usually on from there. He was just being silly. He set the script on fire from the bottom. I wish I had announced it was on fire, instead of making up the temperatures. I think it would have been more effective."

Yes, that one time only, "Miss Monitor" made up the temperatures, while her script was burning. She kept broadcasting as she and Morgan tried to stamp out the fire, and the audience apparently never knew about the conflagration in the little announce booth off the big studio.

What did Tedi really know about the weather? Not as much as she would have liked, at least one time. "I had just given a report on *Monitor,* and after the show, I drove out to Long Island, into the eye of a hurricane. I thought, 'How can this be?'" The explanation was actually simple: The folks at the Washington weather bureau were so used to giving "Miss Monitor" just temperatures and brief descriptions about the cities she asked for that they failed to tell her a hurricane was approaching Long Island.

Tedi Thurman became an immediate hit on *Monitor*. She received "a great deal" of fan mail, mostly from men who asked her for dates, but also a considerable amount from female fans. Her growing fame led her into a juicy television role on Jack Paar's new *Tonight Show* on NBC-TV in 1957. Tedi started doing a funny, sexy takeoff on the weather on Paar's show. "I would wear glamorous clothes and do glamorous scenes" and deliver comedy lines about the forecast. On Paar's show, she was never introduced as "Miss Monitor"—she was always known as Tedi Thurman.

Tedi was a Monday through Friday regular on Paar's show in 1957, and that led to problems for her when *Monitor* expanded to Friday nights in April of that year. *Monitor*, of course, was done at Radio Central in the RCA Building, while Paar's show aired from the nearby Hudson Theater. Once *Monitor* ended at 10 p.m. on those Friday nights, "I would have to run from that studio to the other one (Paar's) to get there on time" for the late-night show's start. Tedi says she never thought of taking a taxi because "it was easier to get there by running"—even on rainy or snowy evenings. No one ever accosted her as she tore through the streets of Manhattan late on those Friday nights—"Those were different days then."

Tedi Thurman was busy in 1957—extremely busy. In addition to performing on the *Tonight Show* and *Monitor*, she was chosen to star in a promotional movie trailer for Dean Martin's *10,000 Bedrooms*. "I had to get permission from NBC to do it. I flew out to California (to film it), and did that during the week and then back to work on *Monitor* on the weekend."

The trailer begins with a picture of an old-fashioned radio with a (very slow) *Monitor* Beacon being heard. On-screen lettering says, "Miss Monitor Tells a Bedtime Story."

The next thing movie-goers heard was "Miss Monitor" giving the temperatures, starting, as always, with Atlanta:

> *In Atlanta, the temperature is 59 degrees, partly cloudy.*
> *Copenhagen, very cold. (NOW MISS MONITOR IS SEEN*
> *SITTING UP IN A BED) One part of the world is getting*
> *warmer and warmer. In Rome, Italy, feminine temperatures*
> *will definitely go up with the arrival of that bachelor with*
> *10,000 bedrooms. (3)*

The trailer features Martin and his co-star, Anna Maria Alberghetti, along with continuing narration by Tedi. The movie bombed at the box office, but at least one critic said the best thing about it was the trailer with *Monitor's* "Miss Monitor."

By this time, *Monitor* executives realized that Tedi was one of the program's biggest, and most recognizable, attractions. She was often used in network promotions and advertising campaigns, some of which involved the creation of records produced for advertisers who had purchased airtime on *Monitor.* The disks were sent out to create excitement for sponsors and their local franchised businesses.

One of them was produced in 1959 for Sacrete Cement. The record cover featured a fetching "Miss Monitor" in an alluring costume. The recording begins with lush music, followed by Tedi's distinctive voice:

> *Come closer. I want to whisper something in your ear. There.*
> *That's better. This is "Miss Monitor," with a secret, just for you.*
> *This spring, I'll be doing more than talking about temperatures.*
> *I'll be pre-selling Sacrete Ready-Mix Cement for you on NBC*
> *Radio's weekend spectacular,* Monitor, *the all-weekend radio*
> *salesman. (4)*

A male announcer follows, saying, "Well, 'Miss Monitor,' I can't think of a better girl to guarantee sales for guaranteed Sacrete."

Life was good for *Monitor*, and Tedi Thurman, from the time the show debuted through 1960. Advertisers had rushed to buy into the program, frequently using Tedi as their announcer—and her *Monitor* appearances made her voice highly recognizable everywhere she went. She got along well with the program's staff members—"We had very good relationships, were all very friendly, very compatible"—and she loved working on the show. "It was always fun. I was never bored." She never took a weekend off.

Tedi was a hit with *Monitor* fans—and her family back home in Georgia vicariously shared in her success. Her niece, Linda Thurman, says the family was thrilled about Tedi and "Miss Monitor":

> *My grandmother had bought this huge Zenith multi-band radio so that we could pick up WSB in Atlanta just to hear Tedi give her throaty forecast. We anticipated her announcing, "And in Midville, it's 90 degrees and sooooooo waaaarrmmm" or some such comment as that. She often tried to mention Midville to let us know she was thinking of us. (5) My grandmother was determined that we would hear Tedi's voice one way or another. Much of the time there was static, but we were all thrilled to hear her. This does give a clue to the family's pride in her success. (6)*

In 1960, Tedi's duties on *Monitor* expanded. "We decided that I would give an in-depth report on major colleges around the country," she recalls. Each week, staff writers researched and wrote several two or three-minute pieces about selected universities. Part of that research involved finding out the students' favorite record—which would be played immediately after each of Tedi's reports.

So in 1960, Tedi was "all over" *Monitor*. But, amazingly, by early the next year, it was all over for her on the program. In March 1961, NBC made radical changes in *Monitor*, cutting its broadcast hours almost in half and reducing the number of staff members considerably. The grand idea of two co-communicators disappeared—one host per segment would be the rule for the rest of *Monitor's* life—and so did "Miss Monitor."

As is often the case in broadcasting, Tedi Thurman never knew she had done her last *Monitor* broadcast until after she had finished it. "I remember we were all shocked," she recalls. "We thought it was going to go forever. I was sad. This was such a wonderful thing. I hated to lose it."

After *Monitor,* Tedi made several guest appearances on NBC-TV programs and appeared on numerous radio and television commercials. She always used her "Miss Monitor" voice for the commercials. She never went back to modeling.

A few years after her departure from *Monitor,* Tedi moved to California and became a successful businesswoman. She would briefly return to New York and then go back to California for good.

To this day—40 years after Tedi left *Monitor*—fans still remember her as "Miss Monitor." Often, at parties, she'll be asked to recreate her distinctive weather forecasts. She always obliges—and always begins, of course, with Atlanta.

Fashion model. Actress. Commercial spokesperson. Businesswoman.

Any one of those would have been enough to proclaim Tedi Thurman a huge success.

But it was her role as "Miss Monitor" that radio fans of the '50s would remember forever. We may not have known Tedi's name, but we knew her voice.

Oh, did we know her voice.

9

The Funny People

Comedy may not have been king on *Monitor*—there were far too many other program elements in each hour for any one of them to be singled out as "most important"—but there is absolutely no doubt that the Kings—and Queens—of Comedy played a major role in the program's success.

Weekend after weekend for years, virtually every big-name "funny person" in show business turned up at Radio Central—either live or on tape—to trade jokes with the communicators or run through part of a routine.

No matter which weekend you tuned in over the course of nearly 20 years, you could hear the likes of Bob Hope, Jackie Gleason, Steve Allen, George Burns and Gracie Allen, Groucho Marx, Dean Martin and Jerry Lewis, Milton Berle, Myron Cohen, Bert Lahr, Buster Keaton, Dennis Day, Jimmy Durante, Jack Benny, Bud Abbott and Lou Costello, Victor Borge, Jonathan Winters, Woody Allen, Phyllis Diller, Bill Cosby and many, many more.

Most of them were "guest" comedians—the people who came to *Monitor* on an irregular basis to chat and joke for just a short time. A few of them—including Winters, Cosby and Diller—performed more frequently for the show.

But when you talk to old-time *Monitor* listeners and staffers about the program's funny people, five names always come to the forefront. These were classic comics who became regulars on the program—they showed up every weekend for years. They, more than any of the others, gave *Monitor* the reputation of being *the* place on weekend radio where you could get a laugh or two.

That reputation started with Bob and Ray. They were the incredibly creative, irreverent duo whom Pat Weaver had hired to "fill time" on *Monitor* when things went wrong.:

> *They had us in a little booth in case of a line failure—they would cut to us and we would do a take-off on what they were going to do. I remember one time, Jack LaLanne (famous physical-fitness buff of the 1950s) was going to swim across San Francisco Bay from Alcatraz with his hands cuffed and rock around his leg. And they cut to San Francisco and there was a line failure, so they turned it over to us, and I remember Bob interviewing me as a Jack LaLanne-type character.*
> *It was great. It was very exciting. Everything was live—no tape. (1)*

Well, not everything—sometimes things went wrong with the tape, too. Hugh Downs recalls one memorable *Monitor* segment in which a taped interview with a musical group had been mis-edited. Downs was supposed to read the questions live, with the answers to be played back on tape:

> *Everything went all right until the fourth question, when I said, "How long have you guys been playing together?" And the answer came back, "Well, we leave that up to our manager, Les."*
> *It didn't seem right to me. I asked the next question and got the same kind of non sequitur. In the meantime, Bob and Ray are collapsing quietly in the studio.*

At one point I said, "I can hear you guys fine, but I'm sure you're not hearing me." Bob and Ray came on immediately afterward and ad-libbed an interview with some bandleader where they did the same thing, just right off the top of their head.

I remember it ended where they said, "Well, it was real nice talking with you, and we hope you'll come back sometime." And the bandleader said, "Fire away with the questions." (2)

Bob Elliott and Ray Goulding—who had first worked together at WHDH Radio in Boston after World War II—had been perfecting their act for a decade before they reached *Monitor*. They created unforgettable characters—basing them on real people they had encountered—and parodied almost every element of American life.

One of their first *Monitor* skits involved two baseball announcers who were recreating a game from a telegraph wire. That was a common practice back in the 1950s, but not the way Bob and Ray did it—as a parody of two popular network radio soap operas:

(SOUND OF TELEGRAPH WIRE IN BACKGROUND)
RAY: Hello again, sports fans, this is Bob and Ray in our telegraphic studio, set to bring you a telegraphic recreation of the big ballgame being played in Elmwood between One Man's Family and Pepper Young's team. Running down the lineup here for One Man's Family—first base, Cliff. Paul will be at second base. Father, catching. At third base, Claudia. Hazel is at short, Jack will be in left field, Panky in center, Pinkie in right field, and on the hill, throwing right-handed, is Mother
(BOB GIVES PEPPER YOUNG'S LINEUP)
RAY: First up now for One Man's Family, Cliff. Cliff bats right-handed.
BOB: Pepper's taking a long windup there, isn't he?
RAY: Here's the first pitch. (SEVERAL SECONDS OF TELEGRAPH SOUNDS)

RAY: Ball one, low and on the outside. At this rate, we'll be here until midnight.

(BOB AND RAY DESCRIBE MORE ACTION)

RAY: I don't understand this at all. The road weather conditions in Mount Washington. Hey, will you check the wire there, fella, there's something wrong here.

BOB: Speed limit seven miles an hour up there?

RAY: No, that's the wrong thing, sir. Look, friends, while we straighten this out, we'll be back with the rest of this game, we hope, as the afternoon wears on. Right now, though, let's return them somewhere in—it's coming in now all right.

Strike two. (3)

There's a funny story behind that funny story. It seems that Bob and Ray couldn't find an ending to that skit. The director kept signaling them to wrap it up, and they kept shrugging their shoulders at him.

Bob and Ray poked gentle fun at almost every aspect of life—even *Monitor*. Once, immediately after "Miss Monitor" finished one of her typically sexy weather forecasts, they ad-libbed a parody of her:

BOB: Bob and Ray back at *Monitor* in New York. A little bit earlier today, we had an Indian guest who was here in connection with the pick-up from Fort Bragg, the parachute jump, and his name is Geronimo. Seems to have taken quite an interest in radio operation.

RAY (USING INDIAN DIALECT): Humn. Here are temperature around Wild West (INDIAN DRUMS IN BACKGROUND)

BOB: We hadn't planned on…

RAY: Whiskey Butte, Montana, 89.

BOB: Whiskey Butte?

RAY: Batman, North Dakota, 103. Loose Noose, Nebraska, 98.

BOB: Look, I'm not so sure we really need this kind of—

RAY: Be quiet. Six Gun, Nevada, 87. Shane, Colorado, 64, degrees. Me have many, many buffalo born in..

BOB: That's the last time we'll book an Indian on this show. (4)

That punch line may be politically incorrect by current sensibilities—but in the 1950s it was taken at face value—it was just funny.

Downs remembers another Bob and Ray skit that he considers masterful:

> *Bob would do the interview and Ray would do the character.*
> *This character was a guy who had invented a nail clipper,*
> *and he wanted to demonstrate it. And this was so subtle, I*
> *wonder how many people got it.*
> *He said he wanted to show how the edge holds up, even*
> *through a full hand. Bob said, "I notice one hand, your fin-*
> *gernails are very long, and the other hand, they're short. Why*
> *is that?"*
> *And Ray said, "Well, I just left it that way so I could demon-*
> *strate how this works on your program." And Bob said, "Okay,*
> *show us." So Ray clipped the first nail and you could hear the*
> *this click, and he said, "You see how evenly that cuts?"*
> *And then he said, "Number two," and the edge is still holding*
> *up. And number three, and he had a comment about that.*
> *And number four. Then he went to number five, clicked it,*
> *and then he said, "Number six," and he clicked that.*
> *And they did it with a perfectly straight face. (5)*

Producer-director Bud Drake worked with Bob and Ray for many years, both on the Mutual Radio Network and on *Monitor.* He loved associating with them:

> *There wasn't much directing when you worked with them.*
> *They just did what they wanted to do. These two guys had*
> *such rapport, they could just ad-lib anything. They didn't*
> *work from scripts most of the time. (6)*

Bob and Ray stayed on *Monitor* until the early 1960s. After the first couple of years, however, they began taping their pieces during the week for playback on weekends. Their *Monitor* material was so good, they won a Peabody Award for it.

For a time in the early '60s, *Monitor* featured not one, but two of the funniest comedy teams in existence. Bob and Ray were still on the program when Mike Nichols and Elaine May were signed to do a series of sketches. It's fair to say that many of the best laughs in broadcasting came during that time from just one program—*Monitor.*

Mike Nichols was born in Berlin, Germany. His family came to the United States when he was seven years old, and he was raised in New York City. He attended the University of Chicago, where he met Elaine May, a Philadelphia native. They discovered a comedy rapport with each other and decided to take it public.

They teamed up to tell jokes at a Chicago nightclub—joined three others to form yet another comedy team—and wound up, a duo again, in New York's Greenwich Village in 1957.

They were in the process of perfecting deadpan dialogue that they used to satirize almost everything they laid their eyes on. They got a big career boost when they appeared on Steve Allen's primetime show on NBC-TV—and became such smash hits that, by 1960, they turned up on the Broadway stage in a show called *An Evening with Mike Nichols and Elaine May.*

And they were on *Monitor,* performing satirical skits that became almost instant classics, like this one. The scene: a typical suburban household.

MIKE (SPEAKING FROM ANOTHER ROOM) Honey, I'm home.
ELAINE: Oh, you're early.
MIKE: Yeah, I got home. I caught the early train.
ELAINE: Good day at the office?
MIKE: Nice day, yes, we got a lot done.
ELAINE: Get a lot done?

MIKE: Murder in the city.
ELAINE: Traffic?
MIKE: Yes, crazy traffic.
ELAINE: There's a lot of traffic?
MIKE: How are the kids?
ELAINE: They're all right.
MIKE: What'd you do today?
ELAINE: Oh, I shopped a lot. And I think they're both coming down with colds.
MIKE: Oh, again?
ELAINE: Yes, and the laundry came back and there's starch in your shirts.
MIKE: Not again.
ELAINE: Just sent them right back.
MIKE: That's the only thing to do, honey, because they'll never learn unless you send them back.

Mike and Elaine continue talking, still from different rooms, about the raise Mike has asked his boss about, and the evening's surprise for dinner, beef bouillon and the "actual beef." Elaine invites Mike into the kitchen to taste the bouillon.

MIKE COMES INTO THE ROOM: All right.
ELAINE (GASPING) You're not Harry.
MIKE: I'm terribly sorry. I must be in the wrong house. (7)

Nichols and May often parodied the medical profession, as they did in this skit on *Monitor:*

MIKE: Come in, Miss Price.
ELAINE: Hello, Doctor.
MIKE: I thought we'd have you sit up today.
ELAINE: Oh?
MIKE: Rather than lie on the couch. There's, uh, something I'd like to talk to you about.

ELAINE: Oh, surely.

MIKE: Now, this may come as quite a shock to you, Miss Price.

ELAINE: What is that, Doctor?

MIKE: Well, I'm afraid I'm giving up my practice. But it shouldn't upset you. Doctor Butterworth is taking over all my patients, a very fine analyst.

ELAINE: I wouldn't want to start with someone else.

MIKE: I've given Doctor Butterworth all your records, Miss Price, and naturally, he will consult with me in the beginning, and he's a very, very highly respected analyst.

ELAINE: Well, is something the matter?

MIKE: Oh, no. I've just—I've given this a lot of thought, Miss Price, and I've decided to give up my practice. I'm going into the movies.

Mike goes on to explain that he was eating in a restaurant when a talent scout saw him. He says he's done a screen test, been offered a seven-year contract and that "your analyst is going to be a star." He says good-bye to Miss Price and then says to himself: "I just didn't have the heart to tell her Butterworth wants to be a fireman." (8)

Unlike Bob and Ray (at least in that team's early days on *Monitor*), Mike and Elaine taped all of their segments. Producer Bud Drake would book three hours a week of studio time at Radio Central and then wait for them to arrive:

> *And they would come in, sometimes an hour and a half late. Sometimes they wouldn't come in at all. But once they came and you got them, they were just marvelous. They might sit there for three hours and enact off-color jokes and not give me anything. Or they might come in and give me 15 pearls in one session. (9)*

Drake says that Nichols and May never came into the studio with any packaged or written material. They'd arrive with an idea—or perhaps take an idea Drake tossed out—and begin ad-libbing lines about it.

They might do 15 minutes on a subject, and I'd have to cut it down to three minutes. It was always a chore to preserve the continuity of the piece and still get the humor out of it. They were very congenial and very willing to listen to me. And if I didn't laugh, they knew they'd missed. They were favorites of mine. I was in awe of them. But I also loved them. (10)

Nichols and May came out with an album featuring some of the material they had created for *Monitor*. It's called *Examine Doctors,* and if you are lucky enough to get your hands on it, you will note that one of the cuts is called "Nichols and May at Work." This is from an unedited tape of a *Monitor* work session with Drake. You will hear Bud's voice asking Mike and Elaine to do a doctor spot.

Nichols replies that nothing funny can be done about doctors. The piece that follows, as well as the entire album, proves him wrong.

Drake says that Nichols and May had a contract to do 500 comedy pieces for *Monitor.* When the contract was up, they left the show. Both went on to great achievements on Broadway and in motion pictures.

Their departure from *Monitor* left a giant gap in the program's laughter department.

Another comedy star who became a *Monitor* regular—and the fifth person long-time *Monitor* listeners remember as being a major contributor to the program—was Ernie Kovacs, who had already established his reputation as one of television's most unique comedians. Kovacs had a live hour-long program on CBS-TV in 1952 and had become the Monday and Tuesday host of NBC-TV's *Tonight Show* when Steve Allen cut back on his appearances. His specialties included satire, slapstick humor and sketches that often had the TV screen go black.

On *Monitor,* his favorite mode of presentation was the monologue:

KOVACS: Greetings and welcome to another session of Mr. Question Man. All questions sent to Mr. Question Man are

analyzed by experts and some of them are read.
Our first question is from Mr. T.W.I. of Gingerbread, Idaho.
He writes: "What animal that lives in Africa has a yellow body
with black spots and a long neck and does not say anything?"
Well, sir, that's a very shy leopard with a long neck. And now
a question from Mrs. N.N.W. from Battle Creek, Wisconsin.
Her letter goes, "Dear Mr. Question Man, I recently won a
prize in a nationwide TV contest consisting of a bottle of
cologne and a free trip to the Antarctic Circle. Since I keep
getting the Arctic and Antarctic circles mixed up and don't
know exactly what to bring in the way of clothing, I won-
dered if you could help me distinguish the two."
Certainly, madam. While the names sound very much alike,
they actually refer to two widely separated areas on the globe.
The Arctic Circle, from the Brazilian word for North Star,
happens to be at the North Pole and is largely uninhabited.
While the Antarctic Circle, after the name of the man who
discovered it, Clifford Circle, is located at the South Pole...if
I were you, I would take along some tropical blouses, shorts,
bathing suites, swim fins, and a parasol, because the South
Pole, being in the south, is naturally very hot. (11)

In 1960, Kovacs was a regular on *Monitor*. He was considered one of broadcasting's brightest stars with an unlimited future. He was killed in a car wreck in January 1962.

Funny people made regular pilgrimages to *Monitor*—often to Radio Central and sometimes in skits recorded during their nightclub routines. One of the comedy regulars was Phyllis Diller—known for her wild hair, raucous laugh and outrageous costumes.

Diller had refined her stand-up comedy routine through years of club bookings before going to New York to appear at the Copacobana. During that booking, she appeared on *Monitor* and was so funny that she was asked to do a series of pieces for the program.

One of her *Monitor* skits was about a Mrs. Clean, supposedly her next-door neighbor in California who did all her housework in white gloves.

> *She gets up at 6 a.m every morning. You know, one of those. She's compulsive. Sweeps her roof. Then she vacuums the lawn, waxes the driveway.*
> *And she won't even allow her husband to take a drink. One night he got really loaded and came home and passed out on the coffee table. She got up the next morning and waxed him to death. (12)*

Another comic who made frequent appearances on *Monitor* was Jonathan Winters. Winters created a multitude of characters and sounds that he showed off to great advantage on Jack Paar's *Tonight Show* and on his own programs on NBC and CBS-TV.

Winters was a *Monitor* regular during the mid-60s. He often would come into Radio Central to record skits with the *Monitor* hosts whose segments would air the routines. Jim Lowe, in particular, has fond memories of those recording sessions:

> *I loved Jonathan Winters. He would come in, totally unprepared, seemingly, and I was his sideman. He would walk in, and I'd say, "What's going on?" He'd say, "Okay, I'm a baseball pitcher from Texas." And I'd say, "Okay, you want me to take it from there?" He'd say, "Yes."*
> *I said, "What's your name?" He said, "Clem." I said, "Now, Clem, you're from Texas, right?" "Yeah, Jim, I'm from Texas." I said, "How did you break into baseball?" He said, "Well, Jim, my brother and me, down there in Texas, we didn't have no money, and we didn't have enough money for balls, so we would throw a dead woodchuck at each other. And that was*

our ball. And that's how I broke into baseball."
And I said, "Well, you've had a brilliant career." You know, I
was just making this up as we went along. I said, "Whatever
happened to your brother? Did he go into baseball?" He said,
"No, Jim, he went into another line of work." I said, "What?"
He said, "He's in jail." And he just made this up as we went
along. He was brilliant. (13)

On *Monitor's* last day in 1975, Winters had one of his creations, Maude
Frickert, talk about the program's demise:

WINTERS (MAUDE) : Oh, I can't begin to tell you the sor-
row that set in when our family heard that NBC Monitor
was going off. You know, we never did get around to watching
the TV.
We've always had the cabinet, but we never had the parts or
the glass. What we did was set our old radio right in there. We
just always listened to everything Monitor ever said.
I tell you, it was tragic. The only other thing was losing our
dog, Spiffy. When we lost the dog—and that was a great
jolt—and then to lose Monitor—I tell you, I've had a small
cardiac arrest over it. (14)

Winters ended his interview by saying he was sorry to see *Monitor* end
and expressed the hope that, somewhere along the line, it would come
back.

The first comedians ever heard on *Monitor* were Bob and Ray, performing live. The last ones ever heard on *Monitor* were—Bob and Ray, on
tape, a re-run of the "soap opera baseball" skit they had originally performed on that first broadcast.

They had started *Monitor* listeners laughing—and they left them
laughing.

And that was no joke.

10

Sponsors and Controversy

Pat Weaver knew that his new sponsorship plan for *Monitor* would make waves. However, it's not clear whether he realized that it would create a firestorm.

All Weaver wanted to do, after all, was destroy the traditional advertiser-network relationship that had existed since the beginning of network radio in 1926. From that time forward, big-name sponsors—or their ad agencies—had "owned" the programs they advertised on. Often those programs were produced by the sponsor—the talent paid for by the sponsor—and the program frequently shifted from network to network, depending on where the advertiser could get the greatest advantage in terms of time period.

Some programs had become so closely associated with their single sponsors that it was almost impossible to think about the show without thinking about the product. For example, Jack Benny's radio program for a time was sponsored by Lucky Strike cigarettes, and the advertising ties were so great that the program was called *The Lucky Strike Program Starring Jack Benny*. Benny and others often incorporated their programs' middle commercial into the body of the show, with advertisers' products playing a part in the plot.

Weaver wanted to change all that. He wanted to wrest programming control away from advertisers to where, in his view, it rightfully belonged—with the networks. Of course, the irony in all this was that Weaver, himself, was a former adman, having worked with the Young and Rubicam advertising agency and for the American Tobacco Company. Now, he planned to turn his back on his old friends and change the way they did business.

What Weaver realized was the old ways of doing that business were dying. Television was stripping the audience away from traditional network radio programs, which had long run in blocks of 15-minutes, a half-hour or an hour. As network radio's audience diminished, so did the effectiveness of the advertisers' commercials—and with that came desperate network efforts to cut their advertising rates in order to keep advertisers on board.

Weaver wanted to create "magazine-style" advertising. In other words, just as an advertiser in a magazine buys a page, but does not own the article that appears next to it, so TV and radio advertisers would buy "participations" on programs controlled by the network without owning that program.

That, thought Weaver, would allow smaller advertisers—the ones without the big budgets—to afford being part of a full-length program—in other words, to get involved with network broadcasting. His *Today Show* on NBC-TV already had incorporated magazine-style advertising—and now Weaver proposed to do the same thing with *Monitor* on NBC Radio.

He outlined his plans in the closed-circuit announcement about *Monitor* to network affiliates on April 1, 1955. First, he admitted that "one of the things that we who are essentially advertising men worry about in radio is the falling away of radio business and the declining use of radio by national advertisers." Weaver said that radio had ceased to be a "must-buy" for advertisers—and that "we aren't going to have 20 ratings any more—you can't build a radio show that's going to pull a 25 rating away from television attractions."

But Weaver pointed out that, if television had been invented before radio, there would still be a need for a strong audio service because people simply can't spend all day, rooted in front of the tube. Weaver then spent several minutes describing the new *Monitor* service, a program, he said, that "enables you to broadcast from our communications center anything of interest or that can be made of interest to the people. In other words, if you don't like what is announced and what is going to play, you know roughly what time it will take and you can come back."

And, he added, *Monitor* would "have more people on it and more important people saying things of high interest and repeatable values than probably anything that has ever been attempted."

Having built up the program, Weaver set the stage for the controversy to follow by describing, in general terms, the advertising sales plan for *Monitor*:

> *A pattern of placing ads at different times and telling the advertiser instead of spending your whole money at a time period that is your own time period, on the old program-spon-sorship basis, you go to a pattern of positions which get over-lapping audiences and adding them all together you will again reach the big audience.*
>
> *On* Monitor *we are planning the flexibility of one-minute, 30-seconds and six-second billboards, really poster ads on radio. This is the result of a lot of work and study on how to make the advertisers come back into radio almost on a forced basis.*

Weaver said that if *Monitor* got the 50 cumulative rating over the course of the weekend that he hoped it would (in other words, half of the nation would hear it), advertisers would be back in the medium to stay. And, knowing that his words, and the *Monitor* plan, would spark heated discussions, he asked for help from NBC's affiliated radio stations:

> *Now this calls for the kind of flexibility in approach by the station managers that they have demonstrated in television over these last five or six years, as we have gone into new TV projects and formats.*

We would never have built what we had built if we had depended upon the old-line patterns. I won't try to sell you on the necessity of the new kinds of advertising now except to say that the boys who are in on these decisions are the former heads of the agencies, of the major agencies, who now work for NBC, and this is advertising know-how at work. We know how the clients operate. We know how the agencies' procedures are set up and what you must do to get the money. And this is what we think you have to do to get the money. (1)

As if anticipating the firestorm to follow, the broadcasting industry's trade "bible," *Broadcasting-Telecasting* magazine, headlined its story about the new *Monitor* service, "NBC Begins Major Revision in Radio Selling, Schedules." The "selling" was deemed more important than the revolutionary 40-hour weekend schedule planned for *Monitor.*

The magazine detailed NBC's sales plans, though stressing that this was unconfirmed information: Ten six-second "billboards" on *Monitor* would sell for $3,000; 30-second commercials would sell for about $700 and one-minute announcements would sell for $1,000. All commercials would be sold on a "magazine" basis, which meant the commercials would air not in any particular time slots but throughout the *Monitor* broadcast (2)

In that same issue, an unidentified NBC affiliate manager said the plan was "just another attempt by NBC to get into the spot business." (3) By that, he meant that the network was encroaching on local stations, which made a considerable amount of money selling commercials to national advertisers who declined to place their commercials on network programs but instead bought air time on a city-by-city, or "spot" basis.

Clarification about the *Monitor* sales plan came in the next issue of *Broadcasting-Telecasting*, which reported that the 30-second announcements would be sold in minimum packages of four per weekend, for a total of $3,000. The prices quoted for all commercials were for the 8 a.m. to midnight portions of *Monitor* on Saturday and Sunday. The midnight to 8 a.m. overnight portion of the show would sell for half the prices quoted. Of course, as was common practice, advertisers who committed to buying more commercials received greater discounts.

In order to induce affiliates to clear (put on the air) as much of *Monitor's* 40-hours a weekend as possible, the stations were given a considerable amount of time for their own local commercials. In so-called "network option" time periods (those hours during which the network could compel the station to put its programs on the air), stations received two one-minute commercial cutaways each hour, plus a five-minute cutaway on the half-hour, which they could use for news and commercials. In addition, there would be station breaks every half-hour.

In non-option time periods, stations received much more time for their commercials—as many as seven "cutaway" minutes each hour, plus the station breaks and five-minute break on the half-hour. (For a period of time in those non-option periods, one-minute station cutaways were not signaled by the *Monitor* Beacon but by a "goo-goo" doll sound. That sound eventually would disappear, and the Beacon would thereafter herald every station cutaway opportunity.) (4)

The sales formula worked. On May 9—more than one month before *Monitor* went on the air—NBC reported that nearly 500 one-minute commercials had been sold for the show. That represented a 138 percent increase in gross billings over the current NBC weekend business. (5) A week later, the network reported that gross billings for *Monitor* up to that point had reached the $750,000 mark. (6)

The weekend before *Monitor* debuted, NBC Radio's entire Saturday-Sunday advertising schedule consisted of only two sponsors: the Allis-Chalmers Company on the *National Farm and Home Hour*, and the R.J. Reynolds Tobacco Company, which sponsored the *Grand Ole Opry*. On opening weekend, *Monitor* was 70 percent sold out, with gross billings amounting to over $1,400,000. More than 1,600 commercial announcements had been sold. Advertisers included the Chevrolet Division of General Motors, Philip Morris cigarettes, the Morton Salt Company, the

B.F. Goodrich Tire Company, the Chesebrough Manufacturing Company, the Gruen Watch Company and Western Union Telegraph. (7)

To trumpet this success, NBC bought an advertisement in the *New York Times* on Monday, June 13—the day after *Monitor's* premiere. That ad quoted several of the sponsors about why they had purchased time on *Monitor.* The head of the Chesebrough Company said that *Monitor* "seems like a good way to use radio more effectively on a high-frequency saturation basis." A Morton Salt spokesman said that "*Monitor* is going to build important family listenership."

And Western Union's president said that "*Monitor's* brand-new programming is an excellent medium for reaching millions of present and potential telegraph customers—while they are on the move or planning to go places."

In that same ad, NBC pointed out that there were more radios in use than ever before—at the beach, in the garden, at the ballpark and on camping trips—and more than 26 million of them were in cars. And, said NBC, "during the non-stop 40-hour weekend broadcasts, they'll be tuned to *Monitor.*" (8)

And what was the reaction to this word that advertisers were making *Monitor* a huge success? The program was called, somewhat ungracefully, a "pig in a poke" by the Station Representatives Association. That group told its members:

> *There's no denying that* Monitor *is cheap, but like a bargain-basement special, you don't know who made it, how long it will wear, or whether it will really fit. A buyer of* Monitor *cannot prove or even approach a reasonable defense of his purchase on the basis of facts.*
>
> *Unfortunately, since it is not known what stations will clear (air* Monitor*), what times they will clear, or much of anything else, and since all announcements float between 8 a.m. and midnight, EDT, blue sky is all that can be used.*

The SRA also said there were no answers to questions such as the time of day a commercial would be broadcast, the audience composition and whether *Monitor* would be a popular program.

The SRA said that even if all NBC affiliates cleared *Monitor*, there were still gaps that spot advertising, not *Monitor* purchases, could best address since NBC Radio had no affiliates in five of the top-50 cities around the country. (9)

What raised the SRA's hackles was that *Monitor's* commercials were being sold at what it considered such low rates that they were driving down the cost of "spot" commercials purchased on a station-by-station basis by national advertisers. That criticism would continue to be made loudly and clearly for years. It would not matter.

On July 18—barely one month after *Monitor's* debut—word came that advertiser purchases of *Monitor* had "fired a sudden enthusiasm in NBC Radio quarters. Consequently, the network now is considering steps to extend its weekend concept of program service."

Broadcasting-Telecasting continued:

> Already the sales record of Monitor has far outstripped the expectations of even its most ardent rooters at NBC. In terms of gross billings for the third quarter (July through September), NBC now has $1,522,000 on the books, representing 1,056 gross minutes of commercial time. The service has been 72 percent sold out on the average. During the July 4 weekend (Saturday and Sunday), the percentage shot up to 97 percent sold out, a feat that is expected to be repeated on the Labor Day weekend. (10)

It was also reported that NBC executives had been conservative about *Monitor's* prospects at first, practically writing off the first three months of its life with expectations of perhaps $150,000 in billings. This meant that *Monitor* had proven to be ten times more effective than originally thought.

And the good news just kept coming. Later in July, NBC reported that *Monitor* contributed an estimated 11-hours and 59-minutes of sponsored time to the network during the first week of the month, which meant that the program was 93 percent sold out. It was also estimated that during the July 16-17 weekend, *Monitor* was 97.5 percent sold out. (11)

Week after week during the summer and fall of 1955, NBC released new facts and figures that showed how more and more advertisers were buying into the program—and making a positive impact on the radio network's bottom line. On August 8 came word that NBC was the only one of the four radio networks to show an increase in gross billings in June of '55, compared to the same month a year earlier. NBC also was the only radio network with increased billings in June '55 compared with the month earlier—while the other radio networks suffered a 13 percent decrease in billings from one month to the next. NBC said one word could account for the increase: *Monitor*. (12)

At that point, *Monitor* was so successful that NBC began serious discussions with affiliates about whether to expand it to weekdays. Some of them complained that *Monitor* cost them spot-advertising business and that it should be called *Monster.* Presumably, they would vote against any such expansion of the program.

The following week brought word that about $200,000 in new advertising business was headed *Monitor's* way. Indications were that the new advertisers included the Scripto pen company, the J.B. Williams shaving cream company and others. At the same time, resistance was said to be building among some NBC stations to any expansion of *Monitor* into the weekday hours. One station chief said the plan would spell the end of his national spot business. (13)

But that didn't keep NBC from forging ahead with expansion plans. In late August, the network announced that its radio affiliates would meet to discuss whether *Monitor* would, indeed, expand to weekdays. *Broadcasting-Telecasting* reported that NBC officials appeared to be in agreement on the desirability of expanding *Monitor's* participating-announcement style of selling to other parts of the week.

There was, however, disagreement about whether the expansion of that sales technique should be made by extending *Monitor* itself to weekdays or by the creation of another program format. No matter what kind of expansion was made, should it come gradually—or all at once? (14)

Before the September 9 meeting could occur, the Station Representatives Association made another public, and very vocal, attack on NBC and on *Monitor.* The SRA again blasted *Monitor's* sales plan, saying that a national advertiser could buy a spot on *Monitor* "at between one-quarter and one-third of what he would have to pay on the station's rate card. If this practice continues and expands, not only NBC affiliates but every other radio station will suffer immeasurably from this depreciation of radio." (15)

NBC Executive Vice President Robert Sarnoff responded to the attack:

> *It is apparently SRA's purpose to foment fear that* Monitor *is endangering station revenue in general, and national spot business n particular. The phenomenal success of many NBC affiliates in selling out the local availabilities in* Monitor— *in weekend time formerly considered marginal—is the best factual answer to this theory.*
>
> *For example, our O and O (NBC's owned and operated) stations…have doubled their sales of weekend availabilities because of* Monitor—*and more than half of these new sales are national spot.*
>
> Monitor *has generated an unprecedented fresh interest in radio on all levels. (16)*

Following the September 9 meeting, *Broadcastng-Telecasting* reported that no action had been taken on NBC's planed expansion—but that the network hoped to put its new program on the air on Nov. 7. Perhaps the most important bit of information at that time came from NBC President

Pat Weaver, who revealed that, in spite of *Monitor's* success, NBC Radio would lose $2 million that year. (17)

One of the most remarkable indications of *Monitor's* impact in getting new network business came not from NBC Radio—but from rival CBS. During the annual CBS affiliates meeting in Detroit that September, much, if not most, of the discussion was about—not CBS programs—but NBC's *Monitor.*

CBS officials went out of their way to downplay *Monitor's* impact and criticize the program. John Karol, a CBS vice president, said *Monitor* was creating "giveaway business" and that CBS was meeting the *Monitor* competition the old-fashioned way—with "programs that attract the largest audiences in network radio." (18) He described *Monitor* as "a seemingly endless succession of unfinished bits and pieces, interspersed by beeps and boops and the pleading admonition to 'take one.'" (19)

CBS affiliate managers were said to be pleased that their network was continuing with its plans for big-name programs instead of a magazine-type strip such as *Monitor.*

That "pleasure" may have been tempered somewhat by NBC's announcement that *Monitor's* gross advertiser billings had passed the $2 million mark and that during the current quarter about 80 percent of *Monitor's* available commercial positions had been sold out. That, said the network, meant *Monitor* had more advertising dollar volume than the weekend business of all the other radio networks combined. (20)

And NBC took out a two-page advertisement in *Broadcasting-Telecasting,* quoting 16 of its affiliates who said that *Monitor* had helped their own bottom line. Among them: WDSU in New Orleans reported it was completely sold out on its weekend commercial availabilities; KSTP in Minneapolis reported that *Monitor* "had the instant effect of stimulating our local business"; WLW in Cincinnati reported its Saturday and Sunday billings were up as much as 300 percent; and WBRE in Wilkes-Barre, Pennsylvania, reported that it had been "100 percent sold out Saturdays and Sundays since June" (when *Monitor* debuted). (21)

On September 26 came word that *Monitor* had chalked up more than $500,000 in gross billings for the period beginning October 1. (22) During that same time, NBC announced that it would, indeed, expand its *Monitor*-type sales plan into the Monday through Friday period—but the program would not be called *Monitor.* Instead, it was named, not surprisingly, *Weekday*—and it would be aimed, NBC said, toward housewives, with features such as childcare, money management, health and medicine and fashions and beauty.

In spite of heavy NBC promotion, *Weekday,* which premiered on Nov. 7, 1955, would be gone within a year—the victim of low ratings caused, in part, by the reluctance of NBC affiliates to fully accept the program and put it on their air.

While *Weekday* would falter and fall, *Monitor* continued to soar. In March of 1956, NBC announced that more than $2 million in new advertising had just been purchased on the weekend show. The advertisers included the Miller Brewing Company, Miles Labs and Quaker State Motor Oil. (23)

By June 1956—*Monitor's* first anniversary—NBC reported that in its first full year of operation, the program had attracted more than 40 advertisers and gross billings of over $4 million. The network said that 4,349 commercials had been ordered during *Monitor's* first year—and that sales on *Monitor* marked a record for weekend advertisers on NBC Radio for the past few years. (24)

The next month, NBC said advertisers would spend 48 percent more dollars on *Monitor* on weekends than with the "second" radio network. Further, it was reported that during *Monitor's* first year on the air, the program had boosted NBC Radio's weekend revenues by 278 percent over the previous year. And, one more indication of *Monitor's* sales success: the program carried 64 percent more sponsored time on weekends than did the "second" radio network. (25)

It was clear to almost everyone that *Monitor* was—in spite of bashing by CBS and the SRA—a huge success with advertisers. Considering that

NBC Radio was still losing money overall, despite *Monitor*, it is easy to conclude that, without it, the radio network would have disappeared.

Monitor had, indeed, gotten off to a flying start, and its advertising success would continue for years. By 1959, *Newsweek* magazine—which called *Monitor* "the biggest thing in radio"—estimated its annual sales revenue at $6 million. (26) The following year, NBC Radio announced that, after eight years of red-ink operations, the network had finally started making a profit. NBC said that *Monitor* would have more than $5 million in billings that year and called it "one of network radio's most commercially successful operations." (27) *Newsweek* said that *Monitor* was "a prime factor in putting NBC Radio in the black for the first time since 1952." (28)

Monitor would continue to be NBC Radio's biggest revenue generator for most of the rest of its broadcast life. By 1966—eleven years after the program's debut—it was estimated that *Monitor* had generated $85 million in revenue—a gigantic amount by network radio standards of the time.

The program had survived intense criticism and scrutiny by naysayers who thought its sales plan spelled radio's doom. From the start, *Monitor* generated selling momentum that would carry it through for nearly two decades.

NBC Radio had millions of reasons to be happy about *Monitor*—many, many millions in terms of advertising dollars and many, many millions in terms of listeners.

11

Making an Impact

Pat Weaver's critics had it all wrong. *Monitor* didn't turn out to be his "folly"—instead, it helped cement his legend as broadcasting's most brilliant practitioner. Clearly, the program became a hit with advertisers—and just as clearly, it was a hit with listeners.

And it became the prototype for a whole new kind of radio that would dominate the airwaves long after *Monitor* had run its course.

In their attempt to "sell" *Monitor* to advertisers before the program premiered, NBC had made a point of talking about the cumulative audience that the program would generate over the course of a weekend. *Monitor's* strength, the network said, would be that people listening anywhere in the nation—at home, on the road or at the beach—could and would tune in.

Monitor was aimed, to a great extent, at the mobile audience. While it was not difficult to measure in-home listening to the program, it was nearly impossible, in the mid-50s, to accurately measure the out-of-home audience. The Nielsen rating service had only recently begun tentative measurements of potential car-radio listeners.

What was known about those who listened in cars was that the ratio of car-listening to in-home listening might go as high as 64 percent across the nation. Specifically, said Nielsen in a September 1955 report, during the previous June between 8:30 and 8:45 p.m. New York Time on Saturdays, 64 percent as many families used car radios as used home sets.

That meant that more than one and a half million families were using car radios. None of them could be measured by any existing ratings system. (1)

Nielsen also reported that the peak period for national car radio usage in June '55 was on Sunday afternoons from 5 to 5:15 p.m., when more than two and a half-million families were using car radios. (2)

What did all that mean for *Monitor?* Just this: Those peak hours of car radio listening coincided with times that *Monitor* was on the air. So NBC, unable to obtain reliable Nielsen figures that would show total *Monitor* listening, was forced into relying, to some extent, on its own figures and assumptions to gauge how many listeners the program had.

In terms of in-home listening, *Monitor* became popular very quickly. The first national Nielsen ratings released after its debut showed that during the 5 to 5:30 Sunday afternoon portion of the program, it was heard in 917,000 homes—making it the third most-listened to program on Sundays during the rating period. (3) In July, *Monitor's* 4 p.m. Sunday segment also placed No. 3 with in-home listeners. (4)

Meanwhile, NBC was hiring its own surveyors to get a more accurate fix on *Monitor's* audience penetration. The network said a survey of car-riders during the last weekend in July 1955 showed that more listeners were tuned to *Monitor* than to all the other radio networks combined. (5) The network also reported that if advertisers bought 15 commercials on *Monitor* and spread them out over a weekend, they would reach 3,670,000 different homes. In other words, NBC said, *Monitor* gave its sponsors far more homes per dollar spent than any weekend sponsor got on the "second" network. (6)

In September 1955, NBC released the results of another special audience survey conducted in major American cities. It showed, the network said, "NBC stations enjoying significant increases in unduplicated weekend audiences." For example, NBC's Washington, D.C., affiliate had a 21 percent increase in such audiences, while its Chicago station boasted a 27 percent increase. Other major NBC affiliates also reported significant increases.

Monitor, said NBC, reached into nearly eight million homes with both radios and televisions and more than five million radio-only homes. (7)

Because of the limitations of ratings services in *Monitor's* early days, it is difficult to accurately tell how many people were listening to the program. However, there is absolutely no doubt that the program was an audience success. One way to gauge that is by the sketchy, special surveys that were done to try to capture car-radio listenership along with those listening in the home.

Another way to measure *Monitor's* audience success is by how NBC's main radio competitor—CBS—responded to it. During the CBS Radio affiliates meeting in September 1955, much of the conversation centered on *Monitor* on NBC. CBS network and affiliate leaders went out of their way to criticize the program—undoubtedly because they were worried about the inroads it had made toward capturing both advertisers and audience.

Yet another NBC competitor— ABC Radio—also gave indirect evidence that *Monitor* was successful. In September '55—the same month the CBS Radio meeting was devoted largely to *Monitor*—ABC Radio announced that it was about to make major changes in its evening schedule.

> *We will shortly announce a programming concept and sales plan that will…find a ready acceptance among listeners and advertisers.*
>
> *Our programming is based on one fact—1955 radio is not 1925 radio or even 1950 radio. Result: Our new programming is keyed to the listeners' needs and the sponsors' media requirements—circulation with frequency, with efficiency. (8)*

ABC later would announce the creation of a series of Monday through Friday "strip" programs—the same program at the same time each night—that it would call *New Sounds for You.* It would be described in *Broadcasting-Telecasting* as "a sort of organized *Monitor.*" (9) It would fail within a few months.

In addition to having at least one radio network attempt to copy it, *Monitor* quickly became one of the most-copied formats in local radio. Just three months after *Monitor* first went on the air, *Broadcasting-Telecasting* reported that local variations of it were springing up "throughout the land."

One of those variations was being done at KLZ Radio in Denver, which launched a *Monitor*-type program in September 1955 that it called *Denver at Night.* This Monday through Friday program aired from 5 p.m. to midnight. A local newspaper described it as "a nomadic microphone reporting the pulse of a big city." *Denver at Night* used the telephone to cover the city and surrounding area for human-interest stories.

The program also gave listeners music, news, sports and a roving microphone that picked up interviews from around the area. The program's opening night sounded as if it took a page right out of *Monitor's* playbook. That evening, *Denver at Night* talked with the new Miss America (who was from Denver) and her parents by long-distance telephone; eavesdropped while a group of Denver orphans said their goodnight prayers; did a remote broadcast from a gas station to discuss recent price wars in the city; talked with local weather forecasters; provided reports from the police and fire departments; aired a conversation with the night watchman at Denver's newest skyscraper; and talked with the radio-TV editors of Denver's two daily newspapers about conditions in London, where they were touring. (10)

Included in the seven-hour marathon broadcast each night were 75 minutes of *Party Line,* in which a master of ceremonies took phone calls and put them on the air.

KLZ's station manager readily admitted that he had copied *Monitor* and given it a local angle suited to the Denver audience. What made that admission even more interesting was that KLZ was a CBS Radio affiliate.

Another station, WTTM in Trenton, New Jersey (this one an NBC affiliate), called its *Monitor* clone *Impulse.* It aired all day on the station—from 6:30 a.m. to midnight. The station manager said he had tossed out arbitrary time periods "and will let the material determine how much time will be devoted to it on the air. The content will determine the form instead of the form determining the content." (11)

Like the Denver station, WTTM used remote pick-ups and telephone calls to cover a variety of local stories. The program was busy during its inaugural week:

> *WTTM during the first week of* Impulse *visited the office of New Jersey Gov. Robert B. Meyner; covered the capture of a murderer (scoring a four-hour beat on all competing media); was on the spot to report the results of the Delaware Valley United Fund; interviewed Miss Pennsylvania; talked to many citizens about flood relief and the peacetime uses of atomic energy; covered opening day at New Jersey State Teachers College; broadcast daily reports from the county agent, live weather reports from the U.S. Weather Bureau and several-times-daily stock market reports. Music, news headlines, ball scores, weather bulletins and on-the-street interviews are interspersed with the* Impulse *specials. (12)*

Yet another *Monitor* imitator had taken to the air in New Brunswick, New Jersey, at station WCTC. There, a program called *Weekend* aired on Saturdays and Sundays from 6:30 Saturday morning to 6:30 Sunday evening. *Weekend* was described as "a running show of news, sports, weather, human interest features, on-the-spot news reports and dance band pick-ups, with recorded music tying the program together." A staff member had been relieved of all his other duties in order to cruise Central Jersey nine hours a day to tape human interest features. In addition, an additional "beeper" telephone had been installed at WCTC's headquarters. (13)

A fourth *Monitor* copycat had sprung up in California, at KHUB Radio in Watsonville. There, *Operation Hometown* was "doing the same job for the audience of this 250 watt station that NBC's *Monitor* does for the network listeners." (14) The station manager said *Operation Hometown* embraced everything:

> *If Johnny Smith has a birthday party, KHUB calls him up, records him from the "beeper" phone and wishes him the best of the day. When an accident happens, the staff member most available covers the event and reports in with the news. It's not just a programming gimmick. We may be strictly corn-ball, but we feel that as a part of the community we should enter into everything. Naturally, it helps business because folks are afraid not to listen for fear they'll miss something. (15)*

Thus, shortly after *Monitor's* debut, it already was influencing the pro-graming of radio stations around the country. Ten years later, *Monitor* would be given credit for being an even greater influence on local sta-tions—it would be called the forerunner of talk radio. And it would still be having a major impact on local stations:

> *My local NBC affiliate (in 1967) was their Pittsburgh owned-and-operated station, WJAS. They had tried one format after another during the '60s without much success. But in spring 1967, someone at either WJAS or NBC came up with a con-cept I don't think anyone else ever did in exactly this way—it was a format for the rest of the station called* Monitor Pittsburgh. *This was an attempt to emulate the network's weekend sound the rest of the time—they used the* Monitor Beacon *sounder and had customized local versions of the then-current* Monitor *jingles cut (the ones that ran at :06, :29 etc). In addition to the usual full-service elements one heard on local radio and the weekday network segments like* Emphasis, *there were other produced drop-ins, some local, some syndicated; and the DJs would identify themselves at the end of segments as "This is Bill Ross at Pittsburgh*

Radio Central," etc., with the NBC chimes on the half-hour and hour. The music was patterned after Monitor's *adult contemporary mix, though I'm not sure how closely. Some of the* Monitor *network hosts, like Brad Crandall, cut promos for the format that ran during the weekend* Monitor *segments ("If you enjoy* Monitor *on weekends, tune in during the week for* Monitor *Pittsburgh.") This format lasted at least a year; in 1969 WJAS adopted an all-talk format that was probably the most successful thing NBC ever did with it (with* Monitor *continuing to air on weekends, of course). (16)*

Monitor also was making a name for itself in areas that might have been impossible to predict before show began. For example, several high-minded journals, including *The Quarterly of Film, Radio and Television,* lavished praise on *Monitor:*

Monitor *had that ants-in-the-pants mobility and immediacy of the American weekend it was designed to enliven. Jazz fans were quickly impressed by panoramic coverage of nightspots from New York City to Los Angeles. Bob and Ray, extraordinary spoofs of excesses in popular culture, found a deserved national audience. Henry Morgan filled in radio listeners on what they hadn't really missed on TV by listening to* Monitor. *In fact, despite its occasionally neurotic pace,* Monitor *had the beginnings of something long needed in American life: a relaxed yet perspicacious criticism of the popular arts. Literate book reviews and profiles on the American theater give another dimension to* Monitor's *coverage of the arts. Indeed, given a little encouragement and constructive criticism,* Monitor *could help substantially to take the hex off "culture" and "the finer things" in America. Its mixture of hammy showmanship and low-key literacy is precisely the means for easing the century-and-a-half cold war in American culture between conscious gentility and aggressive lowbrowism. As it now stands, it remains the best extant hope for a broadcast forum of popular criticism. (17)*

Other academic observers also praised the program. In 1956, broadcast historian Sydney Head called *Monitor* "an ingenious new achievement in network-program flexibility." (18) *Harper's* magazine was impressed by *Monitor*—and by its creator:

Mr. Weaver apparently invented Monitor *to answer the question of what to do with radio now that everybody was watching television. He decided to do this by doing with radio what should have been done with it in the first place, which is to treat it as though it were journalism.* Monitor *is now thriving—even, as they say, "on the commercial side." Smart man, Mr. Weaver. (19)*

The *New Republic's* Howard Becker described *Monitor* as "NBC's gallant effort to revive radio." (20) But there was one critic—award-winning author William Saroyan—who seemed a bit befuddled by at least one aspect of *Monitor:*

A girl coos the weather as if she were standing under the nose of her lover, looking up into his big, blue eyes. What's that all about? There are interviews with very very VERY famous people who just naturally act as if they were no better than anyone else, hardly. There are news reports, baseball scores, new songs, old songs, telephone calls, and the reading of telegrams and cablegrams. As I say, I don't get it yet. Oh, I understand it's a big network trying to hustle up a little business, but why does the girl coo the weather? (21)

How much impact did *Monitor* have on pop culture in America? A whole lot. One indication came in the late 1950s, when NBC had expanded *Monitor* so that it began on Friday nights. That ultra-hip arbiter of all things "cool" (or maybe "hot") in the 1950s, *Playboy* magazine, devoted a full-page cartoon to *Monitor* in which a young lady was seen talking on the telephone to a friend. She told the friend that a certain man had come over for a few drinks on Friday night and that, when she had suggested it was getting late, he asked to stay until the end of the radio program they'd been listening to. The punch line: "Ever hear a thing called *Monitor?*"

What made the cartoon work, of, course, was readers' knowledge that *Monitor* wouldn't end until midnight Sunday.

Another indicator of *Monitor's* impact: Tedi Thurman appeared as "Miss Monitor" in at least one movie trailer—a sure sign that her "cooing" of the weather had made an impression on at least a few people, if not on William Saroyan.

Yet another indicator: In early 1957, *Broadcasting-Telecasting* reviewed NBC's newest entry in late-night television, *Tonight! America After Dark* (the successor to Steve Allen's *Tonight Show* after Steve left). The magazine compared the new *Tonight* with *Monitor:* "Unlike its studio-bound successor, the new *Tonight* races around the country like a sighted *Monitor*...It's an incredible buffet." (22) It is highly unlikely, after the demise of radio's "golden age" in the late 1940s, that any other television programs were compared to radio shows.

Monitor continued to inject itself into America's consciousness in the 1960s. In 1967, Buddy Rich recorded the "*Monitor* Theme" on his album, *Big Swing Face.* That theme, in a shortened version, aired on *Monitor* for several years.

And by the 1960s, *Monitor's* audience had grown considerably. In June of that year, *Newsweek* magazine reported that *Monitor's* listenership was estimated to be 22 and one-half million—this, in a country of 179 million. (23) With today's population of about 280 million Americans, that would be the equivalent of having 34 million listeners every weekend. (The top-rated syndicated radio program in the United States at this writing has about 20 million listeners a week—or less than *Monitor* had 40 years ago with 100 million fewer people in the population.)

In 1964, NBC produced a *Monitor* promotional tape that indicated the program's total audience at 30 million. (24) That seems to have been the high point of *Monitor's* reported listenership. By 1967, NBC was claiming that *Monitor* reached 15 and one-half million adults 18 to 49. Further, the network said that nearly half of all *Monitor* listeners had been to college, compared with only 26 percent of the total American population. (25)

The numbers told an impressive story—during the early through mid-60s, *Monitor* was being heard by an amazing number of people—especially when you consider that by that time, television had completed siphoning off network radio's audience for long-form programs, leaving only *Monitor* and very few other network offerings in existence.

Monitor's impact was felt well beyond mere numbers. Many of those who listened became lifelong fans of the program. One of them was Thomas Frieling.

> *I listened as a kid when I lived in Ohio in the late '50s, driving around in the car with my Dad. And later in my teen years in Birmingham, Alabama, where I believe WAPI-AM ran* Monitor. *I was the only one of my circle of friends who listened—they all thought* Monitor *was square (to use the lingo of the day) and thought I was weird for liking it Okay, so maybe I was, but for some reason it still appealed to me. I guess I really liked the personalities and the ever-changing nature of what I'd likely hear next. And I'd search the several clear-channel radio stations like WLW in Cincinnati to find the late-night segments those times when my local station wasn't taking the* Monitor *feeds. Those were great memories. (26)*

Another *Monitor* fan was Earl Jones, who discovered the Monitorbeacon.com website and wrote:

> *I can't tell you the memories of my preteen childhood (I'm 49 now) that were resurrected by hearing the* Monitor *Beacon and some of those themes that you have montaged on your site. The recording of the Beacon that I've downloaded is a sound that I will keep and treasure forever as a reminder of my growing-up years. (27)*

The Reverend Douglas Drown became a *Monitor* fan early in life:

> *I'm a child of the '50s and '60s—grew up loving Top 40 radio, was an avid fan of Dan Ingram and Cousin Brucie on WABC as well as many other deejays on many other Northeast stations, but for some indefinable reason I always listened to* Monitor *on weekends. Perhaps it was because I appreciated the variety. The program was always interesting, the hosts ("communicators") were witty and great, and the whole enterprise—along with NBC Radio in general—had class. How could I forget those weekend hours spent on WTAG in Worcester with Bill Cullen, Henry Morgan, Murray the K, Gene Rayburn, Jim Lowe, David Wayne and all the others? And how could I forget the legendary, weird but wonderful* Monitor *Beacon and the galloping rhythm of* Night Flight to Madrid *(a popular song of the time) as it introduced the show? (28)*

Another *Monitor* fan, Ralph Gould, got "hooked" on the program early:

> *I first remember listening to the* Monitor *Beacon on my dad's Studebaker radio while he was doing errands in the Boston area. I think it was on WBZ. A couple of years later, we had moved to Phoenix, and I would sneak out*

to the Studebaker to listen to Monitor *on KTAR.
1969 had me working at KCLS in Flagstaff (Arizona) as a
board operator during Saturday afternoon* Monitor *broadcasts. What a treat to be part of the network I had listened to
as a kid! (29)*

Many people wrote to this author about their first experience hearing
Monitor. A common thread that runs through many of those letters is
where that first exposure took place—in their father's car.

That parallels the author's own experience with *Monitor*. Though I first
listened to it on a big, old-time radio in my parents' living room (it was a
Saturday *Monitor* segment hosted by Jim Backus)—I well remember hearing it often in my dad's car as we traveled to and from the mountains for
weekend fishing trips. That we both liked *Monitor* was one of the few
things we agreed on during my teenaged years.

I also remember the day I realized that *lots of folks* listened to *Monitor*. It
happened on a Saturday afternoon—I have no idea what year it was—
when I took my transistor radio with me (tuned to *Monitor,* of course) as
I walked down my neighborhood street.

Throughout the length of that block, I could hear *Monitor* coming
from radios in garages as my neighbors puttered around on that beautiful
summer day. It was incredible.

I thought I was the only person in the world to have had that experience—until the day, nearly four decades later, when a broadcasting col-
league told me he had heard the exact same thing in his Midwestern
hometown when he pushed his baby's stroller through his own neighborhood streets.

Yes, indeed, *Monitor* had impact—a whole lot of it for a whole lot of us.

12

Times Are Changing

Ask anyone who listened to *Monitor* during the 1950s what they remember most about the program, and their answers likely will include Bob and Ray, "Miss Monitor" and how the show kept "going places and doing things"—lots of places and lots of things.

Then ask anyone who listened during the '60s the same question, and their responses probably will center on the hosts—Rayburn, McMahon, Henry Morgan, Cullen, Garagiola, Jim Lowe—and perhaps comedians Nichols and May.

Finally, ask *Monitor* listeners of the '70s what they remember about the program, and you might get a blank stare.

What's the difference between the decades?

In one word, "change"—a continuous series of changes involving almost every aspect of the program. Over 20 years, *Monitor* changed its musical themes, the type of songs it played between segments, its format, its personalities—virtually everything except the Beacon.

Some of those changes occurred because the program became very successful. Some occurred because the program tried to stay successful. And some took place, near the end, in a desperate effort to keep *Monitor* alive.

In most cases, changes were made to induce NBC affiliates to carry *Monitor* when they might otherwise have been inclined to drop it. Because of all the tinkering that took place with the program, the *Monitor* that aired in 1975 bore little resemblance to the program that went on the air 20 years earlier.

Lack of affiliate clearance of *Monitor* was destined, almost from the start, to play a big role in future structural changes in the program. Even before *Monitor* went on the air in June 1955, *Broadcasting-Telecasting* predicted that affiliate reluctance to give up so much airtime to the network would pose a serious problem for NBC. But when the show premiered, that problem seemed to fade away. NBC reported that 150 of the network's 197 affiliates were carrying at least a good part of the 40-hour broadcast. Those not clearing *Monitor* tended to be small stations in small cities. Ironically, the situation would be reversed a couple of decades later—it would be the big stations, and their lack of clearance, that eventually would spell *Monitor's* doom.

The first major problem area that network officials encountered with *Monitor* in terms of affiliate acceptance had to do with the overnight midnight to 8 a.m. Sunday morning segment. In August 1955, NBC officials reported that only 40 to 50 stations were putting that segment on the air. (1) In January '56, that segment was eliminated—thus reducing *Monitor* to 32 hours. An NBC executive said that "the cost of running that show was so expensive, and the amount of stations that were on the air overnight at that point, did not warrant the overnight feature." (2)

Another reduction to *Monitor's* on-air schedule took place over the next year, when the start time for the Sunday morning segment was pushed back from 8 a.m. to 10 a.m. Then in November 1956, NBC officials announced they were considering expanding *Monitor* into the Friday night 8 to 10 p.m. slot and into the Monday through Thursday night 8 to 9 time period. (3) The Monday through Thursday idea was shelved for the time being; but on January 18, 1957, *Monitor* became a Friday night fixture on NBC Radio. That segment had much the same format as the weekend version. On the first Friday night, features included live remote pick-ups of basketball games between Cornell and Columbia and between Maryland

and Georgetown and a horse race from Santa Anita in California. Baseball great Leo Durocher was one of the evening's guests. (4)

The expansion of *Monitor* into the Friday night slot was made to bolster NBC Radio's sagging sales picture. The network still was losing money, and the feeling at NBC apparently was that *Monitor* was one answer. Another answer came from Robert Sarnoff, NBC's president, who urged affiliates to clear, or put on the air, as many of the network's programs as they could. Without that, said Sarnoff, NBC could not guarantee its advertisers the full national circulation that they wanted when they bought network commercial time. (5)

Even with *Monitor's* continued financial success, NBC Radio's bottom line was bleak in 1958. Sarnoff admitted that the network had lost $9 million since 1953. (6) At the same time, NBC's best-cleared program was *Monitor.*

That fact prompted NBC to expand *Monitor* one last time. In April 1959, NBC placed the show throughout its entire nighttime schedule. In addition to its still-massive weekend broadcast of nearly 30 hours, *Monitor* became a Monday through Friday night feature on NBC. On Monday and Wednesday nights, it began at 8:30 and ran until 10. On Tuesday, Thursday and Friday nights, it began at 8 and ran for two hours. (7)

At this point, let there be no doubt that *Monitor* was network radio's most successful show. *Newsweek* estimated its advertising billings at $6 million annually and, indeed, called it "the biggest thing in radio." (8)

Then in late 1959, NBC announced that it essentially was giving up network radio programming except for weekend *Monitor, News on the Hour* and a new series of short weekday programs called *Emphasis.* One NBC affiliate manager called the new schedule a "bikini-type network service. It covers what needs to be covered and leaves us (affiliates) plenty of exposure." The result: *Monitor's* Monday through Thursday night segments were dropped, but the Friday night version remained on the air. (9)

Robert Sarnoff—by then NBC's board chairman—said the new schedule met the "acid test" of a radio network and came after a decade of trying other concepts that had failed. The network essentially was giving its owned-and-operated stations and affiliates time for their own local disk jockeys to play their records and give the time and temperature—except for *Monitor* time on weekends.

NBC Radio's breakthrough year—the year the red ink turned black—came in 1960. In June, officials admitted that NBC Radio had lost $12 million over the past decade. At the same time, they said the network already had $14 million in advertising locked up in 1960, and that *Monitor* accounted for $5 million of that. And by late that year, an NBC vice president said that no further changes or reductions were planned in the current broadcast schedule.

Three months later, that same official, William K. McDaniel, dropped a bombshell: *Monitor* was going to be drastically cut back in its broadcast hours, and its format was going to change. *Broadcasting* magazine headlined it "NBC Radio's *Monitor* Gets Spring Revamp"—and that considerably understated the case. (10)

Monitor's Friday night segment was dropped, and its Saturday and Sunday broadcast hours were cut nearly in half—down to 15 hours each weekend. There would be five three-hour blocks of *Monitor*—Saturdays 9 a.m. to noon, 3 to 6 p.m. and 7:30 to 10:30 p.m. Eastern Time. On Sundays, *Monitor* would air from 3 to 6 p.m. and 7 to 10 p.m. The Sunday afternoon segment would later be increased by one hour—giving *Monitor* the 16-hour weekend broadcast schedule that it would maintain for much of the rest of its life.

In terms of content, the program added personalities Betty Furness, Hugh Downs (he had been off the broadcast for some time), Wayne Howell, Lindsey Nelson, Mel Allen, Bert Parks and Gene Rayburn as hosts either for a three-hour segment or of a series of features covering comedy, news, sports, music and special remotes from around the world. Bob and Ray, Mike Nichols and Elaine May, and Bob Hope would continue to show up for comedy skits.

New features included "Ring Around the World," consisting of commentaries on world developments from NBC correspondents, and "Weekend Report," an in-depth look at the news.

McDaniel said that the changes would place more reliance on NBC personnel and reduce the output of free-lance, or "stringer," news reporters. McDaniel also said that the *Monitor* staff had been bolstered by the addition of a special music supervisor and a script supervisor and by the addition of separate production staffs for each of the five segments. (11)

By this time, the idea of two co-hosts, or communicators, was dead—each segment would be hosted by a single personality. And "Miss Monitor" disappeared from the show.

Why the drastic changes? Years afterward, NBC Radio executive Robert Wogan said in a telephone interview that the biggest reason for cutting back *Monitor's* hours was that station acceptance of it was starting to diminish in late 1960 and early '61. Simply put, the stations were no longer willing to give up so much of their weekend air time to the network when they could profitably sell it locally themselves.

And there was another problem that *Monitor* faced then—had faced for years—and would face until the last segment of the last day it was on the air: the music.

> *It was very difficult pleasing the affiliated stations with the music format. We changed the music format virtually, I would say, roughly every year. Every six months to a year. The (station) acceptances were dwindling from around the country. Not that the show wasn't great. They loved the show, but the music format was a big problem to those radio stations that had now established themselves with specific formats. (12)*

And stations had another gripe with *Monitor*—the length of the interviews. Some stations apparently felt that long interviews with newsmakers and personalities caused listeners to lose interest and tune out. So, Wogan said they demanded, and got, shorter interviews.

The changes in *Monitor* apparently didn't work to NBC's full satisfaction. In late 1961, network chief McDaniel criticized affiliates for failing to give as much support, meaning clearance, to *Monitor* as they gave to *News on the Hour* broadcasts. Still, *Monitor* was fabulously successful in terms of advertising revenue. McDaniel reported in 1961 that the program had more commercial minutes during the weekend than one network had in its entire weekly schedule. (13)

And by this time, Wogan had made another change in *Monitor:*

> *The most important thing, I felt, was that I would use as many television personalities as possible because of the transfer of voice whereby the listener could identify by voice because of the television association. And that's why news people, news correspondents,* Today Show *hosts and quiz people were used on the show. And, also, which was a very important sales tool, was developing specific packages for advertisers. (14)*

Wogan's idea was to hire such stars as Frank Blair (he had not been on *Monitor* for several years), David Wayne, Barry Nelson and Ed McMahon—all of whom were well-known for their television or movie appearances—as hosts for the *Monitor* blocks. Wogan said those changes kept the show alive in terms of station clearance:

> *You lost an awful lot if you did not carry the program. No local station could possibly have conceived or done a local* Monitor *at that point. They were getting national names, recognizable names, voices. (15)*

What Wogan called "an important sales tool," the selling of specific packages of reports to be read by big-name entertainers such as Arlene Francis, Jack Lemmon and others—another *Monitor* staffer, writer Charles Garment, described as a major problem that essentially destroyed the original *Monitor* format of "going places and doing things":

Monitor *was very, very successful, and as a result the sales people were able to sell what they called "packages." Now the packages would consist of a tease line, then a commercial, then a (report), which could be something like household advice or a news spot from around the world, or a comedy spot, and then followed with another half-minute commercial. So the package would run around five minutes. Well, you have a limited amount of time between the opening of the hour. You put in one of these and put in the cutaway (for local station commercials), you come back and you have another package. They started pushing these in so you had one or two in a half-hour, and it got to the point where at some points, all you had was packages. You could barely say anything. There was nothing to comment on. And it cut the (heart) right out of* Monitor. *(16)*

Garment said staff members kept asking the program's executive producer to go to the network vice president "and say, they're killing the show."

And, Garment says, "because *Monitor* was no longer that marvelous, exciting, entertaining place," but instead a program of pre-packaged pieces, more and more stations began dropping the broadcast.

At that point, Garment says, working on *Monitor* was like working on a shoe factory: "You went in, you punched out whatever it was. I could write the whole script in three hours. It was just pathetic." (17)

Wogan attributed the changes in *Monitor* to economics. It had become increasingly more costly to make live remote switches on a regular basis—so those were reduced and replaced with the packages hosted by big-name stars. Thus, the program that had prided itself on going to so many places and doing so many things "was going fewer places and doing fewer things." (18) Instead of "going places," *Monitor* featured more and more personalities. Among those who hosted short reports or special features during the '60s were golfers Arnold Palmer and Doug Sanders, psychologist Dr. Joyce Brothers, satirist-cartoonist Al Capp, and sportscasters Curt Gowdy, Lindsey Nelson, Kyle Rote, Mel Allen, Bill Mazer, Paul Christman, Joe Garagiola and Sandy Koufax.

At the same time the program was using more "big names," it was cutting back on "no-name" staff announcers who used to come in near the top and bottom of each hour to end a segment with *Monitor's* slogan of the moment, such as: "Weekends are different—so is *Monitor,* on the NBC Radio Network." That announcement would be followed by the NBC chimes, signaling the end of the segment and the beginning of local station breaks.

Over the years, other widely known audio slogans included "*Monitor*—going your way, on the NBC Radio Network," "You're traveling with *Monitor* throughout the weekend, on the NBC Radio Network," "*Monitor,* your news and information center," and, one of the last ones, "*Monitor,* your music and information center, on the NBC Radio Network."

By the late-60s, the slogans, and the staff announcers who read them, were no longer a part of *Monitor.*

Meanwhile, the man who had created *Monitor*—Pat Weaver—had long since left NBC. But he was listening on weekends, and he didn't like what he heard:

> *I had listened to enough of (it) to know that they were slipping. They either didn't understand it, or they forgot to read the old memos. But it didn't have the importance that it did. I mean, you didn't have to listen to* Monitor *to know what was going on in the world; and basically, when* Monitor *started, we made a very big point of that. (19)*

Another aspect of *Monitor* that changed many times over the years was the theme music that introduced each hour and half-hour of the program. Some themes remained on the air for just a short time; others stayed for years.

Many *Monitor* fans still have some of those *Monitor* themes running through their heads. One of them went like this: "Don't move, just leave your dial now, here's *Mon-i-tor*. Lean back, and stay awhile now, here's *Mon-i-tor*. On N-B-C."

Another theme was an instrumental called *Night Flight to Madrid*. It was a hard-driving piece that gave listeners the definite impression that something serious and important was about to be heard—especially when it was used to introduce one of Frank McGee's Sunday night *Monitor* shows.

Another theme went like this: "You're on the *Monitor* Beacon, NBC's *Monitor* Beacon…"

And another: "This is *Mon-i-tor*, this is your weekend show. Stay with *Mon-i-tor*, nationwide radio."

And another: "You'll find us good listening. *Mon-i-tor* is on the air."

And one with a country twang: "Well, I'm traveling down life's highway, and things are going my way. I'm happy as a lark and fancy-free. There's good reason why, my friend, my heart's singin' each weekend: I spend time with *Monitor* and NBC."

In 1970, *Monitor* used year-specific themes, including this one: "NBC will be your host in 1970…" (music faded under for a few seconds for the host to speak, followed by singers): "*Mon-i-tor*, radio, *Mon-i-tor* on NBC. *Mon-itor*, radio, *Mon-i-tor* on NBC."

Another 1970 theme: "N-B-C, 1970, babababababa, babababababa, *Mon-i-tor*, Radio, *Mon-i-tor*, Radio"

And another: "From coast to coast, from sea to shining sea, it's *Mon-i-tor* in 1970."

And about this same time, *Monitor* had another theme it played often: "Go north or south, go east or west, just get in your car and you'll head for the best. Wherever you are, you'll find *Mon-i-tor*, on N-B-C."

The problem was, that admirable sentiment was no longer true. By 1970, *Monitor* had hit the wall of affiliate resistance. More and more stations were saying "no" to putting NBC's premiere radio program on the air each weekend—so many, in fact, that *Monitor's* hosts ended a practice that had existed since the show's beginning—mentioning, at least once an hour, specific NBC stations that were carrying the broadcast.

A crushing blow to the program occurred in early '70, when NBC's owned-and-operated station in New York City, WNBC-AM, dumped *Monitor* in favor of local programming. *Monitor* was shifted to WNBC-FM, which had far fewer listeners than the AM station.

That was more than a loss of listeners to *Monitor*—it was a tremendous psychological blow. How could NBC ask its radio affiliates to carry *Monitor* if its own flagship station in New York did not think highly enough of the show to carry it?

The affiliates' reluctance to carry *Monitor* began a vicious cycle that would eventually lead to the program's demise. When a local station no longer carries a network program, that network's commercials become less valuable to advertisers because they aren't being heard in City X or City Y. If City X happens to be a big metropolitan area, advertisers begin demanding and getting cheaper rates for their commercials.

Or sponsors simplify matters by not buying the commercials. *Monitor* began suffering from both problems. It became quite noticeable in the late '60s and early '70s that fewer sponsors were buying into the program's Saturday and Sunday night segments. Often, an entire three-hour Saturday night or Sunday night *Monitor* would go completely un-spon-sored—or have only a very few commercials.

In order to keep too many affiliates from dumping *Monitor* entirely—which would have made it absolutely impossible for NBC to sell the pro-gram—the program began opening up more time for local affiliate commercials. Where, once, the program had started immediately after *Monitor News on the Hour*—now affiliates received a two-minute "win-dow" for their commercials before the Beacon came back to herald the beginning of that hour's *Monitor*.

On Saturday and Sunday nights, NBC opened up a three-minute window after *News on the Hour* and expanded the one-minute internal cutaways for local commercials to two minutes.

Saturday morning *Monitor* with Gene Rayburn remained the most successful segment—it was almost always fully sponsored. Saturday afternoon and Sunday afternoon *Monitor* were moderately successful.

Network officials saw what the future held if they didn't act—and they did. They created a mechanism that either saved *Monitor* or destroyed it, depending on who's talking. The unveiling came in October 1970 at a meeting of the NBC Radio Affiliates Executive Committee in New York.

Wogan—NBC Radio's vice president for programming—started things off by praising the network's weekend show:

> Monitor—*in its 16th year as a program—is still the most flexible format developed. The name remains the same, but the content and personalities continue to change with the times. From all indications, our current hosts, Gene Rayburn, Joe Garagiola, Murray the K, Ted Brown and Jim Lowe, are the most popular hosts ever; and the present format, the most informative and the most relative to our world today. We feel* Monitor *contributes greatly as a means of helping to weld together the world communities (20)*

Then Wogan reviewed *Monitor's* programming for the past year. He said that the program had provided more than 404 news accounts, 610 sports items, 245 stories on drug abuse and health, 72 reports on ecology, 108 inserts on economics and more than 360 celebrity interviews.

In addition, Wogan said, *Monitor* had devoted entire weekends to such topics as the high cost of living, pollution, housing problems, inflation, student demonstrations, drug abuse, unemployment, education, auto safety and more.

He mentioned a continuing *Monitor* problem—the music—saying that the format had been changed just three weeks earlier. The new one featured "one golden standard selection by a popular artist within each half hour of *Monitor*. The remaining selections are current or new or an established hit as heretofore." He said that "excellent reaction" to the change had already been received.

And, Wogan reminded affiliates that just recently they had received 21 additional "availabilities" within the body of *Monitor* so that the locals could sell their own commercials.

Then he brought up the problem that was causing *Monitor* the most headaches: lack of station clearance.

> *Affiliate effectiveness is a two-way street, and in return for your providing us access, clearances if you will, to your daily and weekly audiences, we in turn provide you with access, on a continuous basis, to the events, the people, the music and the ideas from around the world that help attract those audiences. When we do not get the adequate clearances and support from all our stations, then we have a problem both in circulation of our product and in sales. We recognize such a weekend clearance problem exists in some markets mainly because of baseball and football. (21)*

NBC's solution—the creation of "Custom *Monitor*"—a four-part, special pre-feed service that would allow affiliates to clear *Monitor* network commercials and commercial personality and sports segments without putting the entire program on the air each weekend.

It would work this way: On Wednesday and Thursday nights between 7:30 and 9 p.m. Eastern Time, NBC would feed down the network line several *Monitor* services. One would be the "basic commercial" service—all the commercials that were scheduled to air in *Monitor* the following weekend, fed to affiliates in the order of their scheduled appearance on the air. In addition, designated commercial segments, usually between four and five minutes, would be fed. This would include such things as Joe

Garagiola's sports features, as well as reports by Dr. Joyce Brothers, Frances Koltun (*Monitor's* vacation and travel expert) and others.

Stations would be expected to air the *Monitor* commercials and the commercial segments that included the personalities within an hour of the live broadcast time by the network.

Another part of the pre-feed would be timely non-commercial features such as regional reports for theme weekends and news and sports feature material or interviews that might be outdated within five days.

In addition to the pre-feeds, another part of "Custom *Monitor*" was the assurance that future *Monitor* coverage of live sports or news events would be scheduled at regular intervals at 15 or 45 minutes after the hour. This would allow stations not carrying the full *Monitor* service to join at those pre-determined times for a short segment.

Essentially, NBC was begging affiliates to at least put *Monitor's* commercials on their local air, even if they wouldn't clear the entire program.

> *For those stations which find that "Custom* Monitor" *meets their need as an alternative to taking* Monitor *live, it must be recognized that tied in with the complete weekend flexibility of programming which one plan allows, its success depends on the achievement of satisfactory network clearance levels as outlined.* Monitor *now will be available to you in several different forms, and its new highly increased flexibility will in no way jeopardize the actual timeliness of the weekend broadcast by the network. (22)*

The first "Custom *Monitor*" prefeed occurred on Wednesday and Thursday, Dec. 2 and 3. One result was that NBC's owned-and-operated station in San Francisco, KNBR, immediately took the full *Monitor* feed off its air and began airing "Custom *Monitor*" commercials and features around their own local disk jockeys. Thus, at least two of the stations NBC owned—WNBC in New York being the other—did not carry the network's weekend program.

Wogan later said that "Custom *Monitor*" was successful—that "it kept the show alive to many people that would ordinarily not have carried it." (23) Others associated with *Monitor* disagreed. One of them, Steve White, who was in charge of special features and music for the program, said the new idea made it too easy for affiliates NOT to carry it: "The one thing that hurt the show was when it was decided to do 'Custom *Monitor*.' That was the beginning of the end." (24)

Bud Drake, *Monitor's* longtime producer-director, agreed with White, saying "Custom *Monitor*" spelled the "death knell" of the program. (25)

During the early '70s, *Monitor* still relied on big-name hosts and a pot-pourri of feature material each weekend. It remained an excellent broad-cast, as attested by the 1972 Peabody Award it received for broadcast excellence. But listenership had dipped as fewer and fewer NBC affiliates aired *Monitor*. In 1971, NBC estimated that *Monitor* had about 10.5 million adult listeners each weekend—still good, but only about a third of what it had been in the mid-60s. (26)

The commercial deterioration was becoming more and more evident, particularly during the nighttime hours: "It had absolutely no difference as to what we put on Saturday night and Sunday night, you would not get an advertiser to buy it." (27)

By 1973, the situation was getting desperate. *Monitor* needed some magic. Or maybe a miracle. Or perhaps Pat Weaver, riding back into Radio Central on a white horse to save the day.

What it got instead was a rock jock, a shock jock and the Wolfman.

13

Imus and Wolfman to the Rescue?

It was the summer of '73. The Watergate scandal was increasingly bedeviling Richard Nixon's doomed Presidency. In baseball, Hank Aaron was relentlessly hammering his way toward Babe Ruth's "untouchable" record of 714 home runs.

And Don Imus was hosting Saturday night *Monitor.*

If you were a fan of *Monitor's*—if you had listened to it for any period of time prior to 1973—the presence of Imus was, perhaps, the most surprising thing that happened that summer.

What in the world was a "shock jock" who had attended a California broadcasting school—then stayed in the state for his first radio jobs in Palmdale, Stockton and Sacramento before moving to Cleveland and finally to WNBC in New York, all along the way doing wild and crazy things on the air—what in the world was the man who called himself "Imus in the Morning" doing on Saturday night *Monitor?*

This was, after all, the same *Monitor* that many thought was network radio's greatest program. The same *Monitor* that Garroway, Blair, Downs, McGee, Rayburn, McMahon, Cullen and so many, many other big names had hosted. What was Imus doing on *Monitor?*

Trying his best to keep the show alive, that's what. And he was joined in that noble effort by two guys named Morgan and Smith.

No, not HENRY Morgan—his time had come and gone on *Monitor*. No, this particular Morgan was named Robert W. He was a smooth, deep-voiced, slick-talking rock jock who, like Imus, had worked in radio in some small California markets (Carmel, Monterey, Fresno) before hitting the fast track through Sacramento, San Francisco and finally, the state's biggest and richest radio town, Los Angeles, in 1965.

In La-La land, the man who always said "Good Morgan" made his fame and fortune, competing successfully against radio personalities who were so good that they often found themselves hosting network TV game shows or announcing for shows like *Rowan and Martin's Laugh-In*.

As for that guy named Smith—Robert Weston Smith, to be exact—his first radio job was in Newport News, Virginia, and his first on-air name was "Daddy Jules." He started moving up broadcasting's career "ladder," going from Virginia to Shreveport, Louisiana, where he took the on-air name of "Big Smith." By 1964, he'd moved south of the border, to Del Rio, Texas, where, on XERF Radio, a powerhouse with 250,000 watts, he changed his name one last time.

He became Wolfman Jack.

A year later, he'd moved his name and act to XERB near Tijuana, Mexico, where night after night for years, he introduced rock and roll records in such an unforgettable voice and made such unforgettable comments that he became, in the Southwestern United States, a radio legend.

And then, in the summer of '73, that legend spread worldwide when the Wolfman played a role in *American Graffiti*, the movie that is said to have defined an entire generation of Americans.

Imus, Morgan and the Wolfman—all chosen as rotating as hosts of Saturday night *Monitor* in the summer of '73. It was NBC's last-ditch attempt to save nighttime *Monitor*, which had, over the past few years, seen most of its commercial inventory disappear as advertisers simply abandoned evening network radio.

So Saturday night *Monitor* became an experiment—one that lasted from June until December of '73. From 7 to 10 p.m. each Saturday night (the show's start-time had been moved up to 7 p.m. several years earlier), Imus, Morgan and the Wolfman were turned loose in a talk and music format. While maintaining the Beacon as the show's trademark, their programs broke away from the traditional *Monitor* format. Musical sensibilities—always a problem for *Monitor*—went out the window as each DJ played rock and roll records that never would have been allowed on the program in earlier years.

On *Monitor*, Morgan—Robert W.—presented the most "traditional" style of the three. He remained the smooth, suave performer that Los Angeles had so eagerly embraced when he was king of the hill there. He spiced up his *Monitor* segments by taking lots of "live" phone calls from big-name celebrities such as Sinatra Senior (the calls were actually on tape, but who knew?) and aptly handled the variety of *Monitor* introductions and duties demanded of any host.

Wolfman Jack was, well, Wolfman Jack. He used the same gravel voice that had helped skyrocket him to fame. He made some of his same wild comments. He was about as far removed from a traditional *Monitor* host as anyone could imagine.

And then there was Imus. On *Monitor*, he called himself "Imus in the Morning, in the Evening, on *Monitor* '73, on NBC." As he did on his local morning show on WNBC Radio in New York, Imus brought to *Monitor* a variety of "characters" he'd created to spice up his presentation. One of them was known as Judge Hangin'—who had the distinction of being able to perform while dead. The judge often reminded listeners that "the law is our friend, and anyone who hurts our friend, should be beaten senseless," and that "police brutality is the fun part of law enforcement. It's a way for them to work off steam."

After the judge's comments, singers would inform listeners that he was "110 percent American, are you?"

Another Imus creation was a preacher named the Rev. Billy Sol Hargis, who headed up the "First Church of the Gooey Death and Discount House of Worship" in Del Rio, Texas. This man of God often sold such items as a Holy Land Record Package, which included acts like Him and His Disciples (recorded at the Last Supper) singing "For He's a Jolly Good Fellow." Listeners could also send for information on how to operate their own drive-in church and baptismal car wash.

One of Imus' recurring gags was called "Imus in Washington," in which he made up news reports about current events:

> *Our report today is on the possible future of Richard Nixon. This is one possibility. The day after tomorrow, the Senate Watergate Committee and the Security Council of the United Nations will meet in joint session to declare that upon Richard M. Nixon's resignation from the White House, he will crowned, sitting on a snow-white camel, Effende Red Ree-shard, monarch of a newly created state in the Sinai serving as a buffer between Israel and Egypt... Or how about this. The day after tomorrow, Nixon stops his Senate trial with the announcement of the invasion of the USA by a combined force of Martian and Albanian troops. He accuses Algier Hiss, Myrna Loy, Archibald Cox and Col. Huexe of conspiring with 3,000 UFOs. (1)*

Imus lampooned everything in sight, including himself. Once, after announcing a record that had just aired on *Monitor,* he said the song's writer was a friend of his:

> *He didn't give me anything to play it. It was already a hit. Although if it hadn't been a hit, I would have taken some-thing to play it, I'll tell you that.*
> *Who would say something like that dangerous on the air-waves? Imus in the Morning, in the Evening, on Monitor '73, on NBC. (2)*

Imus also interviewed a broad range of entertainment people and generally brought a sense of wild energy and mayhem to *Monitor.*

NBC made a big promotional push during the Saturday night experiment, primarily centered around Imus. He was featured in a full-page NBC promotion sent out to affiliates. It was headlined, "Now mighty mouth of the morning moves to *Monitor* and the nation":

> *The most outrageous, irreverent, hilarious, overall-clad dude trucked into New York last year to put WNBC Radio on the charts as the number one wake-up station in the metropolitan area—and he's doing it. His name? Don Imus, better known to millions of early-morning New Yorkers as Imus-in-the-Morning. He calls himself "What you call your GREAT Imus in the Morning." (Well, no one ever called him humble.) Due to the fantastic response to Imus-on-*Monitor one Saturday night, Don Imus has been awarded the* Monitor *Saturday Night Show once a month. (3)*

The promotional piece featured letters from *Monitor* listeners about Imus. One said, "We'd like to suggest instituting Imus as a permanent Saturday Night *Monitor* host." Another listener wrote, "Please give us more of Imus. Sure would be great to hear him every weekend." And a Michigan listener said that "certain people in this town went bananas when you showed up on *Monitor.*"

While Imus, Morgan and the Wolfman held forth on alternating Saturday nights the rest of the year, NBC was struggling for answers to *Monitor's* sagging clearances and diminishing advertising. Among the stations not carrying *Monitor* anymore were NBC's owned-and-operated outlets in New York, San Francisco and Chicago. Why didn't NBC officials simply call those stations and order their managers to put their own network's programs on their air?

> *That was not our thinking at all. That was not our management thinking, and rightfully so, because many stations,*

including the owned-stations, would say that they could not succeed if they were forced into carrying something that was not their image. And I think at that point management wanted the owned-stations to succeed and was not about to force them into taking any of its network programming. (4)

In June of '73, network affiliates received a report about a recent NBC Radio Executive Committee meeting, in which *Monitor* had been discussed.

Network executive Robert Wogan had reported that *Monitor's* music would be "toned down." (This was prior to the Saturday Night *Monitor* "experiment" with Imus and Company.) He noted that both "Custom *Monitor*" and the regular *Monitor* stations "remain very enthusiastic" about Guy LeBow's sports segments and a PGA golf series. He said the network's greatest recent successes had included recent big-band specials hosted by Art Ford on *Monitor*.

Favorable reactions were reported from affiliates to recent changes in *Monitor's* music, though the report warned that "the diversity of (station) program formats may make it impossible to entirely standardize music." The report said that "NBC should continue to strive for a broader, more balanced mix of (*Monitor*) program material, including more information of interest to listeners in the Midwest and Far West as well as the East."

And one line in the report to affiliates—one that could easily have gone unnoticed—indicated the depth of *Monitor's* clearance problem. "Many affiliates favor eliminating the *Monitor* title on weekend newscasts." (5)

In other words, many affiliates were making it known that, since they did not air *Monitor*, they no longer wanted their weekend *News on the Hour* to have a different sound than their weekday versions. Weekend news, for nearly two decades, had started with the *Monitor* Beacon and had been known as *Monitor News on the Hour*.

During this time, at least one NBC Radio affiliate—the one in Sacramento, California—went out of its way to eliminate any vestige of *Monitor* on its weekend air. In addition to not clearing the program, the station would "cover up" the Beacon that started *News on the Hour*. Instead, the station played a tape version of the weekday hourly news theme, then joined the weekend newscast "in progress." As one might expect, the "join" usually took place when the newscaster was in the middle of a word or sentence.

In October '73, word came that *Monitor News on the Hour* was about to die. Russell Tornabene, NBC Radio's vice president and general manager, sent a notice to affiliates that starting November 3, all *Monitor* identification would be dropped from the weekend newscasts. In other words, *News on the Hour* would have the same theme seven days a week. What this meant was that stations not carrying the full *Monitor* program would no longer have anything on their air that referred to the show.

That Sacramento station wouldn't have to bother playing a taped open any longer.

At the same time *Monitor's* theme came off the weekend hourly news, NBC cut back that newscast from five and a-half minutes to five minutes. With a two minute-10 second music "fill" after the weekend hourly newscast, *Monitor* would begin at 7-minutes-10 seconds after the hour.

But it would be a different type of *Monitor*—because when NBC announced changes in *News on the Hour,* the network also told affiliates that starting November 3, 40 live news and sports reports would be broadcast at 15 and 45 minutes after each hour on weekends. That was an effort to get affiliates not clearing the full *Monitor* show to at least join the network at a quarter-past and a quarter-to the hour.

The new segments were to be called *NBC Update*. They would effectively cripple *Monitor's* format because they required the Beacon cutaway for local-station commercials to hit on an exact-time basis—at 13:50 and 43:50 after the hour—so that the *Updates* could air on a real-time basis at 15 and 45 after the hour.

To illustrate the extent of *Monitor's* new problem: The Beacon now came up at 07:10 after the hour, leaving only 6 minutes and 40 seconds of program material available before the mandatory Beacon at 13:50 after the hour. Two records, a little patter and maybe a commercial or two were all *Monitor* could put into that segment. The script for new host Big Wilson's first *Monitor* program illustrates the point (courtesy of Gene Garnes Jr.)

DISC:	CRUNCHY GRANOLA SUITE (PERCY FAITH) (ESTAB AND UNDER FOR ID)	
BIG (OVER)	(I.D. OR ANYTHING ELSE THAT GRABS YOU)	
DISC:	UP AND FADE ON CUE	
9:07:10		
CART:	OPEN THEME (RUNS :18) (ESTAB FOR :02 UNDER FOR ID)	
BIG:	Monitor...the new Monitor...I'm Big Wilson...and I'm going to be your Saturday morning host from now on.	
CART:	BOOS	
BIG:	Gee...I didn't expect that.	
CART:	APPLAUSE	
BIG:	Now that's what I expect...so let's get it on...new...Dawn.. "Who's in the Strawberry Patch With Sally."	
DISC:	WHO'S IN THE STRAWBERRY PATCH (SNEAK :01 1/2)	
TAPE:	DOOR BIT O: BIG WILSON AGAIN C: THAT'S ALWAYS OPEN (DOOR OPENS	(2:15)
(MUST HIT AT 12:15)		
CART:	ALKA SELTZER COMM	(:30)
CART:	HOLIDAY INNS COMM	(1:00)
BIG:	And another "in" place to be...on weekends, is right here...on the friendly Monitor beacon	
(MUST HIT AT :13:50!!!)		
BEEPER		
DISC	CUTAWAY	
(BEAT)		
CART:	UPDATE OPENING	
NEWSMAN:	UPDATE CL: "THIS HAS BEEN NBC UPDATE"	(approx 1:20)
CART:	UPDATE CLOSING	

Tornabene also announced that *Monitor* was being "restylized" and would have a new line-up of personalities, new production techniques and bright "middle of the road music." And he added that the changes were merely the beginning of a "major up-dating of the NBC Radio Network."

He promised that "interesting new program concepts" would be announced as soon as research was completed. (6)

What NBC had essentially done was tear *Monitor* apart and put only part of it back together again. Gone were existing hosts; gone was the Saturday night experiment with Imus, Wolfman and Robert W. Morgan; gone was *Monitor's* capability to let the content dictate how long a segment would go because everything had to be programmed around the *Updates* at 15 and 45 after the hour.

Later that same month of October, Wogan responded to a letter from a worried *Monitor* fan who had heard about NBC's pending changes and wondered about his favorite program's future:

> *You are quite astute in your observations of our program changes on the NBC Radio Network. I can assure you that every attempt is being made to maintain the* Monitor *program, although as you yourself have noticed many changes in style and format have taken place. (7)*

Another change in "style"—for both *Monitor* and the entire NBC Radio Network—was reported in the *New York Times* on November 1:

> *The National Broadcasting Company's chimes, an audio trademark since 1929, are being eliminated for a new, more modern sound.*
>
> *The NBC Radio Network will continue to herald its programs with three notes, but there will be new and different musical versions for* News on the Hour *and each of the other programs, including* Emphasis *and* Monitor. *(8)*

And the changes just kept on coming. On December 14, NBC dropped yet another bombshell on *Monitor*. Beginning the first weekend in January 1974, the program was cut back to just six live hours each day. Gone were the Saturday and Sunday night live segments.

Monitor's new live Saturday broadcast hours would be from 9 a.m. to 3 p.m. Eastern Time, with six hours of re-runs to follow from 3 p.m. to 9 p.m. The 9 a.m. to noon live hours would be repeated from 6 to 9 p.m. that night, while the noon to 3 p.m. live hours would be aired again from 3 to 6 p.m.

A slightly less complicated schedule would appear on Sunday. Live *Monitor* would air from noon to 6 p.m. on Sundays, with the noon to 3 p.m. hours repeated from 6 to 9 p.m.

As NBC put it:

> *The revised schedule eliminates original programming in the evening hours and adds two hours of new programming from 12 noon to 2 p.m. Sunday. By repeating the second program block Saturday in the 3-6 pm time period, we are providing the same program service that is offered in daytime* Monitor *at present.*
>
> *The service will end one hour earlier on Saturday in order to provide continuous service to stations taking the program in blocks and in order to provide consistent service on Saturday and Sunday. The new schedule also contains much greater flexibility for carrying the program.*
>
> *There have been two objectives in our efforts concerning* Monitor: *to improve the quality of the program and to achieve better station acceptance. We feel from listener response and response from stations that we have made progress in the first area—improving the quality of the program. But station clearances are a continuing problem. These further changes are an attempt to deal with another of* Monitor's *persistent problems—not one of quality but of quantity. By adopting this schedule, we are reducing the number of original program hours from 16 to 12 for a more efficient and effective program instrument. (9)*

Along with that memo, NBC sent out a grid sheet with helpful hints on how affiliates could, perhaps, program *Monitor.* The part with suggestions for programming Saturday *Monitor* segments looked like this:

NYT	SEGMENT	SOME OPTIONS FOR STATIONS CARRYING MONITOR						
		1	2	3	4	5	6	7
9-10 am	A	A	A			A	A	A
10-11am	A1	A1	A1			A1	A1	
11-12 noon	A2	A2	A2			A2		
12-1 pm	B	B		B		B	B	B
1-2 pm	B1	B1		B1			B1	B1
2-3 pm	B2	B2		B2				B2
3-4 pm	B repeat		B		B			
4-5 pm	B1 repeat		B1		B1	B1		
5-6 pm	B2 repeat		B2		B2	B2	B2	
6-7 pm	A repeat			A	A			
7-8 pm	A1 repeat			A1	A1			A1
8-9 pm	A2 repeat			A2	A2		A2	A2

There were, NBC assured its affiliates, many other scheduling variations for Saturday that they could develop for themselves so they could take the *Monitor* feed without using their own tape machines to record the program for later playback. In other words, the network was asking—begging—its affiliates to take this program—please—in any form at any time they could. But, in case they still didn't—the "Custom *Monitor*" pre-feed of commercials was kept in place.

What NBC had effectively done, of course, was to destroy *Monitor's* ability to have any live, on-the-spot coverage of events during the body of the program. Because the repeat hours had been introduced, the program no longer could go to the scene of a breaking news event because that event very likely would be outdated by the time the repeat segment aired. The program that had "gone places and done things" was now out of that business.

Network executive Steve White admitted the obvious:

We became a little more specialized in the kind of interviews
we would do. Obviously everything was limited because of the
length of time as compared to the old days. Things were cut
down to keep the show moving, try to make it more compati-
ble with stations with top-40 formats or stations that were
also programming on an upbeat basis. (10)

Producer Bud Drake felt the changes in the program's content and
broadcast schedule resulted in a definite deterioration of the product:

The show was nowhere near as entertaining, or diverting or
informative. It was just a disk jockey show, expanded a little
bit beyond the edges to include a little bit more information.
(11)

The new *Monitor* would also have a new executive in charge. Over the
program's nearly 20-year history, it had only a few executive producers:
Jim Fleming, Frank Papp, Al Capstaff, Marx Loeb and Bob Maurer. Now,
Maurer, who had been at *Monitor's* helm since 1962— left abruptly.

Monitor's new hosts for the new schedule were "Big" Wilson, Tony
Taylor, Bruce Bradley and John Bartholomew Tucker. They would preside
over a format that consisted primarily of music and recorded interviews
with celebrities.

In April 1974, Wilson and Tucker became the only two regular
Saturday and Sunday hosts. Network officials made the decision to use
just two voices because, they said, "the use of the same hosts Saturday and
Sunday will give *Monitor* a consistency of sound on the weekend that stations seek in their weekday programming." (12) That move was the last
major effort NBC would make to revive a sagging *Monitor*.

And Big Wilson and John Bartholomew Tucker would go down in
Monitor's history as the last hosts the program ever had.

14

The Beacon Fades Out

Sunday, January 26, 1975. What had been a radio revolution was about to die at NBC's Radio Central on the fifth floor of the RCA Building in midtown Manhattan.

You would not have read about it in the *New York Times*—no matter where you looked. The death of network radio's greatest program apparently did not fit into the *Times'* umbrella of "all the news that's fit to print."

That day, on Page 1 of the *Times,* the lead story dealt with the world's major oil-producing countries agreeing to hold a meeting in a few weeks to decide what to do about the price we all pay at the pump. Other front-page stories included one about the Republican Party announcing a comeback plan with a television and voter drive; one that said President Ford was found to be in "excellent" health after a four-hour checkup; and another about how New York City police were searching for two men seen running from the Fraunces Tavern annex moments before a bombing there the previous Friday left four patrons dead and 53 injured.

The weather in New York that day was expected to be partly cloudy. (1)

At Radio Central, Pat Weaver's critics were finally about to be proven right. They had called *Monitor*—his radio baby—"Weaver's Folly." They said it could never work. They said it would never last. They said it would fail.

And now, 19 years and seven months later—after more than 1,000 weekends on the air and over 20,000 hours of broadcasts (far more than any network radio show in history)—they were about to be proven correct.

All *Monitor* had done during that time was bring NBC millions of dollars of revenue and millions of listeners and, to put it bluntly, keep its radio network in business—and now it was, as Weaver's critics always knew it would, going off the air.

After all the major changes that *Monitor* had gone through in the past year, what had happened to bring it to this point—to the point of death?

One of those occurrences was the appointment of Jack Thayer as president of NBC Radio in July.

Another important event was actually a non-occurrence—changes the network had made in *Monitor* apparently had no impact on local affiliate station acceptance of the program.

It wasn't that NBC didn't try to make the show work. The network essentially had turned *Monitor's* broadcast schedule into a pretzel in an effort to get stations to put some part of it—any part—on the air. And if stations didn't put *Monitor* on, maybe they'd put those *Updates* at 15 and 45 after each hour on the air.

But the stations quickly gave the *Updates* a "thumbs down," and by the summer of '74 they had been, thankfully, stripped away from the 15 and 45 positions and put on the half-hour. Now, *Monitor* could at least have a little more flexibility in programming its segments without regard to the mandatory "hits" at a quarter-past and a quarter-to each hour.

And what *Monitor's* new executive in charge, Lee Sherwood, did was turn *Monitor* into a disk jockey show—a classy one, to be sure, but essentially a fast-paced DJ show with short—very short—interviews and segments. Sherwood loved having "theme" weekends or segments that explored various aspects of pop culture. One such segment, in February, dealt with the movie *The Exorcist* and featured interviews with the writer of the book and the film; the film's director; plenty of interviews with the film's stars, movie critics and people who had seen it and some audio clips from the movie.

As Sherwood put it in a memo to affiliate stations: "The documentary is not a plug for the movie but rather an in-depth look at one of the most talked about, popular phenomena of our times." (2)

During the weekend of March 9 and 10, *Monitor* went hog-wild over the Grammy Awards that had been presented the week before. All weekend long, the program featured the music and winners from the awards.

> *Stevie Wonder, who won four awards for: "Album of the Year," "Best Rhythm and Blues Song," "Best Rock Performance-Male," "Best Rhythm and Blues Vocal Performance-Male," and whose album* Innervisions *won an Engineers Award, will talk with Big Wilson in the Saturday, 9 -12 noon NYT segment (repeated 6-9 p.m. NYT).*

Each of *Monitor's* other segments and hosts had a similar description of the stars and music that would be featured during their three live and three repeated hours. And there was more:

> *In addition to the winners, our regular personalities, Jean Shepherd, Pomerantz and Finkelman and Dr. Joyce Brothers will also center their spots on the Grammy celebration theme. (3)*

On the weekend of March 30 and 31, *Monitor's* theme was money— how to save it, make it stretch, hold it and guard it:

> *Highlights of* Monitor's *"Money Saving Special": Among our guests will be Vivian Cadden, senior editor of* McCall's, *on 50 Painless Ways to Save Money. Morton Shulman, millionaire author of* Anyone Can Still Make a Million, *with suggestions for unusual investments. Peter Bird Martin, senior editor of* Money *magazine, with last-minute tips for making*

out your taxes. Dale Remington, vice president of New York
Travel Writers, on cheap but chic travel. Bernard Gladstone,
home improvement editor of the New York Times, *with sav-*
ing money on home repairs. (4)

And, there would be more: Those regular *Monitor* contributors, Dr.
Brothers and comedians Pomerantz and Finkelman, would also focus on
money.

NBC's next big announcement about *Monitor* came in a memo to affiliated stations on April 3. Two of *Monitor's* four surviving hosts—Bruce
Bradley and Tony Taylor–were finished:

Beginning this weekend, April 6th and 7th, Big Wilson and
John Bartholomew Tucker will take over as the regular
Monitor *hosts in both the Saturday and Sunday segments.*
The two have a compatibility of style that will give Monitor
its own distinctive character throughout the weekend. Also,
the use of the same hosts Saturday and Sunday will give
Monitor *a consistency of sound on the weekend that stations*
seek in their own weekday programming. We are pleased that
John and Big have been so heartily welcomed to the Monitor
host lineup this year, and we hope this will build further on
their familiarity and success with the Monitor *audience. (5)*

So *Monitor's* future now rested on the shoulders of just two on-air
men—and for at least one of them, they were broad shoulders, indeed.

"Big" was certainly an appropriate name—and description—for
Wilson. While he was on *Monitor,* he weighed 310 pounds—and joked
about his capacity for food. NBC's press release described him this way:

Big is no stranger to broadcasting—nor does he qualify as a
"newcomer" to the radio scene. Before his distinctly fresh and
vital sound was heard over NBC Radio, he was an emcee/disk

jockey at stations in Scranton, Pennsylvania—Philadelphia,
Cleveland and Plattsburgh, New York. (6)

Curiously, that press release left out Big's biggest radio job—he had
been both the morning man and the mid-day host on NBC's owned-sta-
tion in New York, WNBC. In fact, he had been there for 11 years and had
established himself as one of the city's most important disk jockeys.

Of course, his work on WNBC might have been left off NBC Radio's
announcement about his *Monitor* duties because Big was in the process of
being fired from WNBC. His last day on the air there was March 15,
1974. He exited the station with class and dignity—and, though it was
hardly solace, with a bit of revenge, just a short time later: The ratings
came out, and Big Wilson got the satisfaction of knowing that he had the
top-rated program during his time period in New York when WNBC
fired him.

On *Monitor*, Big was pleasant, upbeat and a constant ad-libber. He was
"quick" on the air—fitting *Monitor's* needs-of-the-moment for a fast-
paced program—and an easy-listen for anyone who happened to tune in.

He was also easy to work with—no big ego, for this giant of a man:

> *He was an awful nice guy. He was very congenial. Biggie had*
> *such a common-man touch. There was no "la-de-dah" or any*
> *airs about him. He was just a substantial, honest, entertain-*
> *ing guy. (7)*

Monitor's "other" last host may have been slightly better known than
Biggie. John Bartholomew Tucker had worked as a radio disk jockey in
Springfield, Massachusetts, and Binghampton, New York, before moving
into television and hosting entertainment/variety programs in Baltimore,
San Francisco and New York. For a short time, he hosted a network TV
game show, *Treasure Isle.*

One of the things *Monitor* fans of that time probably remember most
about Tucker was his voice. He did not have those deep, bass tones so

prevalent in the early days of network radio. Instead, he had a rather high-pitched tone that he used to perfection on the air—often to make jokes about the material he introduced or about himself.

The other thing fans remember about Tucker on *Monitor* was how he reacted after a particular pop music hit of the moment aired. The piece was Maria Muldauer's *Midnight at the Oasis*, a rather sultry creation with sexy lyrics in which she suggested slipping "off to a sand dune, real soon" to "kick up a little dust." And that was the least-suggestive part of the song.

Every time Tucker heard it—and it was played often during his segments—he would ad-lib a response indicating that, indeed, he wished he were stranded in the desert with the desirable Maria. It became a Tucker signature of sorts over several months on *Monitor*.

But no matter what Wilson or Tucker did, it would be another person who would make a far bigger impact on the show.

The announcement of Jack Thayer's appointment as president of NBC Radio was made to affiliates on Friday, July 12, 1974. In a closed-circuit message, NBC President Herbert Schlosser said that "Thayer's creative leadership will extend the growth and progress of our radio division." (8)

Thayer came to NBC after more than 30 years of experience in radio and TV. NBC's announcement said he had been "personally identified with many of the significant and progressive developments in the radio industry over the past three decades."

Thayer's first words on the closed-circuit feed were, "Hello, NBC—it's showtime!" He expressed his pleasure at being chosen head of the network and said he planned to listen closely to affiliates in order to find out their needs and desires. He also said that "profit is not a goal at NBC Radio—it is a requirement." (9)

There is no doubt that Thayer faced a rough road on his way to profit. He admitted that his radio network—after making money in the early '60s—was again losing "as radio networking generally has lost money for 10 years or so." (10) Indeed, *Business Week* was saying that the NBC Radio division had lost "heavily" for years. How many years, exactly, is a mystery, since the network itself had not commented on radio profits since 1969, when then-president Arthur Watson said that NBC Radio had made money in that year. (11)

Monitor staffers now had two reasons to be worried about their program. First, their new executive producer had changed the program's format drastically:

> *What he wanted to do was not* Monitor. *He was doing a pop-music show. They were doing anything they thought might keep the affiliates hanging on to us, but by the same token, they were killing the show. There was no longer a* Monitor *continuity. (12)*

Second, there was concern about what the new network radio president thought about *Monitor,* though some thought they knew: "Jack Thayer used to send us (staffers) notes saying, 'Great show. On your side.' Signed, Jack." (13)

Thayer liked *Monitor* so much, he decided to kill it. That word went out on December 4 to affiliates in a closed-circuit message sent not by Thayer, but by Russ Tornabene, the radio network's vice president and general manager. He began his announcement not by mentioning *Monitor,* but something else:

> *Jack Thayer, president of the NBC Radio Division, will be making a public announcement tomorrow that a new and expanded weekend service of news, news features and live sports reports will begin in February 1975. The new weekend service is part of an overall restyling of the network service and will replace the long-running* Monitor *program. As for* Monitor, *in its nearly 20 years on the air it has made a significant contribution to news, information, sports, entertainment and public service as an integral part of the American scene, and an important part of NBC Radio's total service.*

> *Jack Thayer points out that though* Monitor *itself will no longer be a part of the program schedule, the pioneering spirit which spawned* Monitor *and the valuable precedents which it set, will evidence themselves in all our future efforts. (14)*

Thayer later would report that the decision to end *Monitor* was made after numerous discussions with affiliate station officials.

The *New York Times* reported *Monitor's* pending demise the next day in a story headlined, "*Monitor* to End on NBC Radio; 'Restyled' Network Service Set." The story alluded to *Monitor's* persistent problem of recent years: lack of station acceptance of the program:

> *Occupying sizable blocks of time on Saturday and Sunday,* Monitor *had been considered an anachronism by many NBC Radio affiliates in a time when most radio stations require little more than news on the hour from a network. Many stations have felt that their acceptance was weakened, rather than strengthened, by a network service that disrupted the continuity of their regular programming, which in most cases is a musical format. (15)*

Broadcasting reported that at the end, *Monitor* was heard on about 123 stations—or about half of NBC's network affiliates. (16)

Network executive Bob Wogan, who had worked with *Monitor* for years, thought the program's demise was inevitable:

> *Anything that's successful is going to dwindle after awhile, if only because that station is going to find, if it's successful, he's going to sell more and more locally. He needs more and more time. So if anything has to suffer, it's not going to be his dollar—it's going to be our (network) demands. (17)*

Steve White, who had worked on special projects on *Monitor,* agreed with Wogan: *Monitor* could not be saved.

*I think as we lost certain markets (cities), especially like New York and our other owned-areas, I think that was really just the handwriting on the wall. Nothing goes on forever. And some of the other great shows didn't even have a long run like (*Monitor*); they weren't on for 19 years. (18)*

But what did *Monitor's* creator—the man who designed it and put it on the air in the face of critics who said it could never last—what did Pat Weaver think about the announcement of *Monitor's* demise? He hated it.

The stations would have been lured back (to Monitor*) if the format was very much in the stations' interest. If it looked like they were going to get money from station compensation from the clients, if it looked like the segments that they were going to cut away from, if it looked like they could sell all of those at a good price because the show was being talked about and being listened to, and the ratings were good enough, of course they'd come back. They're selfish, that's all they (station owners) are. (19)*

And Weaver—who, during his long career never shied away from saying exactly what he meant—pulled no punches in his description of how NBC should have handled *Monitor:*

The first thing they (network officials) should have done, if the show was really in jeopardy as evidently it was in the last year or two, the first thing they should have done was to call me up and say, "Will you review Monitor *for us and see if we can update it and upgrade it and get it back where we can clear the stations we're losing and get the advertisers back?" (20)*

Weaver's anger—expressed in a personal interview with the author a couple of years after *Monitor* left the air—was matched, if not exceeded, by a prominent New York City talk show host a few days after word had come of *Monitor's* cancellation. In an extraordinary move, Barry Farber of WOR Radio—not an NBC affiliate—devoted one of his programs to *Monitor.* He called it "the pinnacle of broadcast perfection, provocation, excitement, really everything that exemplifies that which American broadcasting is capable of." He continued:

> *I am proud to come from a country that could spawn* Monitor, *and I question the changing values of a country where the network that spawned* Monitor *20 years ago can say,* "Sorry, we're canceling Monitor *for a restyled network service."*
>
> *What it means is that one rock-and-roll record after another on the hundreds of stations that make up this network is somehow more profitable, and therefore more compelling, and therefore more desirable, and therefore more inevitable, than the collected talent of the National Broadcasting Corporation to take us around the world regularly at any given minute on a weekend. (21)*

Two things—lack of station clearance and the subsequent lack of advertising—had doomed *Monitor.* If NBC stations in major cities did not air the program, advertisers were reluctant to purchase airtime on it. Apparently, even "Custom *Monitor*" had failed at the end to induce stations to at least air the commercials.

How bad was the sponsorship situation? Very. The weekend before Christmas 1974—a time when *Monitor* traditionally had been full of commercials in years past—provides one key example. That weekend, the always heavily sponsored Saturday morning 9 to noon segment had 28 commercials. However, for the entire three remaining *Monitor* segments that weekend, only 13 commercials aired. (22)

The commercial schedule for the following weekend was even lighter. Only 22 commercials were spread out over *Monitor's* 12-hour live broadcast schedule. True to form, the vast majority of them—17—aired on Saturday morning *Monitor*. The Saturday afternoon segment had no commercials at all, and Sunday afternoon's 3 to 6 p.m. segment had only one. (23)

It got a lot worse near the end: On the weekend of January 4 and 5, 1975, the only *Monitor* segment that had any commercials was (of course) Saturday morning's, with 10. The other three live *Monitor* segments had no advertising at all. (24)

Longtime *Monitor* writer Charles Garment says that, once *Monitor's* pending death was announced, program staffers asked network executives for a favor: "We were hoping we could do one final 'real' *Monitor* show to say goodbye, but they wouldn't give us that." (25) What he and others wanted to do that last weekend was the type of *Monitor* that had aired in the '50s—a program that "went places and did things" again. A program that had lots of live elements instead of pre-packaged features. A program that sounded exciting.

NBC said no.

But in spite of that turndown, *Monitor's* last programs, on the weekend of January 25 and 26, 1975, provided a magnificent look back at some of the highlights of a wonderful 20-year life.

Included were new interviews with many of *Monitor's* former "communicators," or hosts, as they were later called, including Dave Garroway, Hugh Downs, Frank Blair, Ben Grauer, David Wayne, Barry Nelson, Ed McMahon, James Daly and Jim Lowe; classic *Monitor* comedy skits by such mainstays as Bob and Ray, Nichols and May and Ernie Kovacs; and fresh interviews with comedians Bob Hope, Phyllis Diller and Jonathan Winters.

Other highlights included a Dr. Joyce Brothers "session" with Don Imus and a bit of double-talk artist Al Kelly's *Monitor* routines.

Former *Monitor* executive producer Marx Loeb called in from Tucson, Arizona, where he assured host Big Wilson that *Monitor's* signal was coming in loud and clear. Not so clear—at least, on the concept—was the early-day *Monitor* "stringer" who was heard struggling to end his report with the appropriate "now back to *Monitor* in Radio Central." He had finally gotten it right, but it took several tries.

And there was music—plenty of music from the '50s, 60s and 70s, all of which had aired on *Monitor* over the years and much of which illustrated the problem the show always had in satisfying its affiliates. Some of NBC's old-time stations undoubtedly cringed whenever such rock hits as *Rock Around the Clock* aired on the same program as *Theme From a Summer Place* and *Aquarius*.

And there were the *Monitor* contributors who had meant so much to the program over the years. One of them, movie critic Gene Shalit, turned his final *Monitor* piece on that last Sunday into a cultural retrospective, reminding listeners about some of the movies and books that were popular on the program's premiere Sunday so long ago—June 12, 1955. Among the best-selling books of the time: *No Time for Sergeants* and *The Power of Positive Thinking*.

Movie-goers, Shalit reminded us, had their choice of such hits as *The Blackboard Jungle*, Disney's *Lady and the Tramp*, *The Seven-Year Itch* and *Marty*. And, he said, the movie-makers were having some worries in June 1955:

> *An article in the* New York Times *on June 12, 1955, bemoaned the fact that the stars the studios had been thriving with, were getting too old to play the parts that were being written. Major studios had at least 25 scripts, according to the story, 25 scripts that they could not find big-name actors for. What's going to happen, they said, now that old favorites like Gary Cooper, Joan Crawford, Clark Gable, Spencer Tracy, Barbara Stanwick, Humphrey Bogart, Katherine Hepburn, James Cagney, all these people they said, were just about washed up. Ah, little did they know. But, the article said, we have these newcomers, and maybe these newcomers will be able to make it. Among those*

mentioned in 1955 were Jack Lemmon, Marlon Brando, Leslie Caron, Jean Simmons, Richard Burton and a girl named Marilyn Monroe.
Well, that was pretty good guessing. (26)

Shalit concluded his last report by saying:

Who could guess that Monitor *would endure for almost 20 years? It has, and most of the time it was fun. And now for the last time, I'm going to say, this is Gene Shalit for* Monitor. *(27)*

And there was Joe Garagiola, one more time, on *Monitor.* Joe had done double-duty for the program—he had served as both a host and as a sports reporter. Not just "a" sports reporter—the program's premiere sports guy, doing more than 2,500 reports over the years.

His final one was a tribute to the men and women of *Monitor:*

This is a tough one for me, for it marks my final appearance on Monitor. *This is the last day, after nearly 20 years, for one of the real great ones in the history of American radio,* Monitor. *The cliche in this business is to leave 'em laughing, which is a great philosophy. But I honestly don't feel that way right now. I'm going to miss* Monitor, *both as a broadcaster and as a listener. And there's another side to my feelings on this day, too. Along with millions of you people, I think about* Monitor *as the voices you heard. But I also recognize* Monitor *as the voices you never heard. The people who made it all possible. The executives, the writers, directors, producers, engineers, assistants, and everyone else whose contributions were so important to those of us whose voices you did hear. I shared a lot of great moments with those people. They fixed up my fluffs—and there were plenty of them. They shared the laughs that people who work together get to share. And they also amazed me when they showed me how professionals act in moments of stress. I tell you, they made me very proud to be a member of their team. And now comes the time for me to say to them, and to you, so long. And it's the last time I'll do it here on* Monitor. *I'm copping out by mentioning no names. But that isn't as bad a feeling as I'd get if I overlooked somebody. And besides, over a dozen years, you build up a lot of people to thank. To all of them, thank you. You made it fun. And also, you have given me, through your efforts, a feeling of pride, every time I got to say, as I do now for the last time, this is Joe Garagiola for* Monitor *sports. (28)*

Another long-time *Monitor* contributor who made his last report on that final Sunday was newspaper columnist and author Bob Considine. His radio feature, "On the Line," had showcased him reporting on some of the world's biggest events for years for both *Monitor* and other NBC Radio programs.

I was able to come up on Monitor *from the ends of the Earth. From newspaper assignments as varied as the Korean War, to the death of Pope John XXIII, the World Series, the launching of a missile, a long interview with (Soviet premier) Khrushchev from Moscow, with Bob Denton, good old Bob, speaking for my sponsor, Mutual of Omaha. Ah, those were the days, my friend. But what the heck. It is better to have loved them than never to have experienced them at all. It was great deal of fun.*
And with great pride, I used to say, this is Bob Considine for Monitor. *(29)*

But the most poignant moments that last weekend came from *Monitor's* hosts, Wilson and Tucker. At 12:07:10 p.m. Eastern Time, Wilson began his last three-hour shift on *Monitor* by saying:

> *This is the show I didn't want to get here. Well, it's here. The farewell program on* Monitor. *And I'm Big Wilson. Hi, it's nice to be with you. We're reminiscing about the many years—well, almost 20—that we've been on the air. Many of the people who have been with us as hosts, or as contributors in other ways, will share the program today. It all began on June 12, 1955. (30)*

Three hours later—at 2:58 p.m.—he followed Considine's last report by playing a bit of *Sentimental Journey* and then said:

> *As Bob Considine said, those were the days. Those were the weekends, the innumerable weekends, when anyone listening to radio anywhere in the country, could be entertained and informed by scores of people striving to make this program a superior source of entertainment and information. And I've been happy to be a part of it all. This is Big Wilson, with thanks to all of you, from* Monitor. *(31)*

Then NBC's new "chimes sound" rang out, and at 2:58:50 p.m. Eastern Time, Big Wilson's brief career as a *Monitor* host came to an end.

A few minutes later, at 3:07:10 p.m. Eastern Time, John Bartholomew Tucker began his final *Monitor* segment—and the last live three-hour *Monitor* segment ever—by saying:

> *Well, hello there. This is John Bartholomew Tucker, and this is* Monitor.
>
> Monitor *on NBC has been on the air for more than a thousand weekends. And this is our last show. Happy to have you with us.*

*And this is one of the songs we played for you in 1955, our
first year on the air.* Mr. Sandman, *by the Chordettes.* (32)

The program's last three live hours featured interviews with comedian
Phyllis Diller and with former *Monitor* hosts Nelson, Blair, Grauer and
Garroway. Former host Frank McGee's memorable interview with civil
rights leader Martin Luther King Jr. was heard, as was Garroway's classic
chat with entertainer Eddie Cantor.

Monitor's creator, Pat Weaver, was heard in a taped interview that
Tucker introduced this way:

> *Were it not for a man named Sylvester L. "Pat Weaver," there
> never would have been a kaleidoscopic phantasmagoria
> known as* Monitor. *Mr. Weaver, who was the president of
> NBC, conceived the idea for the program and the term
> describing it, a kaleidoscopic phantasmagoria, was attributed
> to him.* (33)

Weaver and Tucker discussed network radio's problems in the mid-50s
that had led Weaver, almost out of desperation, to create *Monitor*—and
Weaver expressed sorrow about the end of his radio "baby":

> *I'm saddened that the show is going off the air because I think
> that such a show could be done and, run properly, would con-
> tinue and be effective both for the network and the stations
> and the advertisers. But I think really, you've done very well,
> and I'm only saddened that all of you aren't going to have*
> Monitor *there anymore.* (34)

Tucker expressed the staff's admiration for Weaver:

> *That was Sylvester L. "Pat Weaver," the man who formulated
> the* Monitor *concept and who had the imagination to put it
> on the air. We all admire him. We wish him well.* (35)

The last live hour that *Monitor* would ever broadcast began with the Beacon at 5:07:10 p.m. Eastern time on January 26, 1975. After *Monitor's* newest (and last) theme aired (it was simply a four-second "sounder" without lyrics, in keeping with NBC's philosophy of "keep it fast-paced"), Tucker said:

> *Well, hello there. This is* Monitor. *John Bartholomew Tucker here. Big Wilson and I bringing you this, sadly, the last day of* Monitor. *We've invited a lot of old friends back for our farewell party. (36)*

In the hour that followed, Tucker talked with Garroway about the former communicator's interview with Marilyn Monroe and with John Chancellor about his early days as a *Monitor* roving reporter out of Chicago.

Monitor's last guest was one of its first hosts—Hugh Downs, who bantered with Tucker about the "old days" of *Monitor* when things used to go wrong and when Bob and Ray were at Radio Central, ready to make light of, and bring laughter to, those mistakes.

The end of that interview went this way:

TUCKER: You feel right at home again, don't you?
DOWNS: I sure do, yeah. I feel like I ought to do a commercial or station break.
TUCKER: You want to just say, "This is Hugh Downs on *NBC Monitor*"?
DOWNS: It would be a great pleasure. Give me a cue
TUCKER: It's been awfully nice talking with you, sir.
DOWNS: Thank you, John. This is Hugh Downs on *NBC Monitor*. (37)

A few minutes later, *Monitor* played the last bit of music that would ever air on the program. This time, there would be no difficulties in having stations worry about whether it was "too much" for them, because that last song was a four-minute original musical tribute to *Monitor* written and performed by the legendary Sammy Cahn:

Monitor *first came around in 1955, it's been a long, long time.*
And it had a brand new sound, 'cause Monitor *was live, it's*
been a long, long time.
And every doubter soon became a true believer, so here's a bow
to our-then prez, Pat Weaver.
For 20 years old Monitor *has managed to survive, it's been a*
long, long time.

Cahn sang about such *Monitor* personalities as Garroway, Clifton Fadiman, Frank Gallop, Ben Grauer, "men we think of with affection to this very day." Nichols and May, Bob and Ray, Phyllis Diller, Marlene Dietrich—all received Cahn's accolades.

And then came the end:

I can't believe that 20 years are now behind us,
And it took four choruses to remind us.
It's Auld Lang Syne for Monitor, *so sing it loud and strong:*
It's been a long, long time, it's been a long, long time. (38)

Then Tucker closed *Monitor:*

Thank you, Sammy Cahn. What do you say after that except,
thank you. It's time, my time, I guess, to say goodbye to all of
you listeners who have become friends of this program in its
nearly 20 years of existence.
We leave you reluctantly. We leave you, we hope, with some
indelible memories. We certainly have them.
This is John Bartholomew Tucker. And you'll never hear this
sound live at this hour again. This is Monitor *on NBC. (39)*

The Beacon played one last time, followed by NBC's traditional chimes from *Monitor's* early days.

And so, at 5:58:50 p.m. Eastern time on Sunday, January 26, 1975, the Last Great Radio Program ended, leaving behind memories—oh, so many of them—that would live forever for millions of us.

Epilogue

The death of *Monitor* made news around the country. On Monday, January 27, 1975, the Associated Press ran a story about it:

> Monitor, *the weekend news and entertainment series on the NBC Radio Network, now is only a memory. It'll be replaced next weekend by a series of news broadcasts and live sports reports.*
>
> Monitor, *which in earlier years was heard up to 16 hours each weekend in three and four-hour segments hosted by a prominent personality, began in June 1955. The final show was on Sunday.*
>
> *Last December, NBC said it was taking the series off the air to provide what it called "a more contemporary feel" to its weekend radio schedule. (1)*

The Associated Press made one glaring mistake in the article. In its earlier years, *Monitor* was heard up to 40 hours each weekend—not the 16 the AP wrote.

The *Washington Post* played that wire service story on Page B3 on Wednesday, January 29. The *New York Times* did not run the article or any mention of *Monitor* after the program's demise.

A few weeks after the final *Monitor* broadcast, NBC Radio sent its affiliates a colorful packet of information about its plans for new programming that it would call the *NBC News and Information Service* (NIS). It would consist of network news programing that would fill 50 minutes of every hour, seven days a week. For those affiliates not wanting to take this service, the network would program its traditional *News on the Hour.*

Because network programming at that time was distributed by telephone "land lines," NBC could have only one program at a time coming down those lines. Thus, in order to make way for its all-news, all-the-time format, the network had to get rid of weekend *Monitor* to "clear the lines."

By late 1977, NIS was dead—leaving NBC Radio with little more than *News on the Hour* and a few sports broadcasts—and I was finishing a masters thesis about *Monitor.* A copy went to Pat Weaver, the program's creator, who had so kindly opened his home to me months earlier for an extensive interview about the program.

He disagreed with my conclusion, in the thesis, that *Monitor's* demise was inevitable at the time, given the then-disastrous state of network and AM radio. He wrote:

> *Like most reporters, you accept current conditions as realities developed by circumstances beyond management control. Not true.*
> *Radio can serve the present audience. Network function can be useful and profitable to the public, stations, advertisers and creative community. But it requires an intellectual and professional solution when things change.*
> *This could have happened with* Monitor. *Pity that the NBC management was, in this case, as in most, without some basic knowledge of advertising (where the money all comes from), programming (where the audience comes from) and even station realities (all stations will go for audiences, income, prestige and public service).* Monitor *could have been reshaped.* (2)

Apparently, *Monitor* nearly DID come back, in the late '80s. NBC Radio put together a study group to look at the possibility of putting it back on the air. Things went so far that audition tapes of the new *Monitor* were made.

Then General Electric—NBC's new corporate owner—decided to sell off NBC Radio and the network's owned-and operated stations. With that sale went any chance that *Monitor* would return.

Could *Monitor* work today? Its fans like to say "yes," but there are doubters. One of them is Bob Maurer, who was the show's longest-tenured executive producer.

> *Absolutely not. Because local radio is much too important. Talk shows on local radio are much too important. You can't do talk shows on national radio like you do on local shows. (3)*

Bud Drake, *Monitor's* longest-tenured producer, isn't sure whether *Monitor* could come back:

> *I think a show like it could work, but you'd have to persuade the stations to carry it. Stations now are all into DJ's and local news and that kind of thing, so there are very few radio stations that need the kind of help that* Monitor *gave them. (4)*

Charles Garment, one of *Monitor's* long-time writers, points out that *Monitor* is on the air now—but in a different form and on a different network. He compares *Monitor* with National Public Radio's long-form evening newscast, but only to a point: "They call it *All Things Considered.* They don't have all the things that we (*Monitor*) considered 'all things.' We had music, we had everything." (5)

In October 2000, this author established a commemorative website for *Monitor* at http://www.monitorbeacon.com. The expectation was that the site would generate perhaps a couple of hundred "hits" in its first year.

By October 2001, more than 9,000 hits had been logged, and the author had received hundreds of letters from former *Monitor* fans who expressed their thanks. They told their stories about listening to *Monitor* and explained how it had, in many cases, changed their lives.

And many of them said they'd listen again if *Monitor* ever returned to the air.

Perhaps one day they'll get the chance—the chance to again "go places and do things" with a big-time sounding program that keeps its audience in instantaneous touch with anything interesting going on anywhere in the world.

The chance to hear, again, a distinctive sound that everyone will know heralds the start of the program.

Who knows—maybe they'll call the show *Monitor*. And that sound—maybe they'll call it, a "Beacon."

We can only hope.

Chronology

1955   On April 1, Pat Weaver and Jim Fleming announce *Monitor* plans to NBC Radio affiliates.

On Sunday, June 12, *Monitor* premieres with 4 p.m.-to-midnight specialbroadcast. First hour is simulcast on NBC-TV.

On Saturday, June 18, regular *Monitor* program debuts at 8 a.m. and runs continuously for 40 hours until midnight Sunday.

1956   *Monitor's* midnight to 8 a.m. Sunday morning hours eliminated.

On September 7, Pat Weaver resigns as chairman of NBC and leaves network.

1957   *Monitor* expands to Friday nights from 8 to 10 p.m.

1959   *Monitor* expands to Monday thru Thursday nights.

1960   *Monitor* eliminated from Monday through Thursday night NBC schedule.

1961   *Monitor* drastically cut back to 16-hour weekend schedule.

Dave Garroway leaves *Monitor* and *Today Show.*

1965   *Monitor* celebrates its 10th anniversary. Sammy Cahn and Jimmy van Heusen stay in Radio Central all weekend to write a birthday song that Steve Lawrence performs live.

1974   In January, *Monitor* reduced to 12 live hours each weekend

In December, NBC announces that *Monitor* will end the following month

1975   *Monitor* has final broadcasts on January 25-26. Final hosts are Big Wilson and John Bartholomew Tucker

1977   Ben Grauer, the first voice heard on *Monitor,* dies

1982   Dave Garroway, *Monitor's* most prominent early host, dies

1987   Discussions underway at NBC Radio about bringing back *Monitor.*

1988   NBC Radio and owned-radio stations sold by General Electric

1990   Bill Cullen, *Monitor* host and contributor, dies

1994   Henry Morgan, longtime *Monitor* host and contributor, dies

1999   Gene Rayburn, *Monitor's* longest-tenured host, dies

2000   In October, *Monitor* Tribute Pages established at http://www.monitorbeacon.com

2002   *Monitor—The Last Great Radio Show*, published

Monitor Hosts Year-by-Year

Pat Weaver called his *Monitor* hosts "communicators." From 1955 to 1961, each *Monitor* segment had "co-communicators," or two hosts. Below are the regular hosts for most of *Monitor's* segments from 1955 to 1975 (all times Eastern). Not shown is the midnight to 8 a.m. Sunday segment that lasted only seven months–it was co-hosted by Al "Jazzbo" Collins and Leon Pearson. Also not shown: Sunday's 8 a.m. to noon segment, often hosted by Gordon Fraser, Gene Hamilton and Al Capstaff; and Sunday night's 10 p.m. to midnight segment, hosted frequently by Gene Hamilton or Mel Brandt. (Of course, there were frequent "guest" hosts of all segments–they are not included in the charts.)

		SATURDAY			SUNDAY	
8 a.m.-noon	Noon-3 p.m.	3-6 p.m.	6-10:30 p.m.		2-6 p.m.	8-10 p.m.
			1955			
Frank Blair	Hugh Downs	David Brinkley	Morgan Beatty		Clifton Fadiman	Dave Garroway
Frank Gallop	Gene Hamilton	Don Russell	Walter Kiernan		Ben Grauer	Don Russell

		SATURDAY			SUNDAY	
8 a.m.-noon	Noon-4 p.m.	4-8 p.m.	8-midnight		2-6 p.m.	7-10 p.m.
			1956			
Frank Blair	Hugh Downs	David Brinkley	Monty Hall		Frank Gallop	Dave Garroway
Don Russell	Peter Roberts	Walter Kiernan	Morgan Beatty		Gordon Fraser	Don Russell
			1957			
Frank Blair	Hugh Downs	Walter Kiernan	Monty Hall		Ben Grauer	Dave Garroway
Don Russell	Peter Roberts	Johnny Andrews	Morgan Beatty		Frank Gallop	Don Russell
			1958			
Frank Blair	Hugh Downs	Walter Kiernan	Monty Hall		Ben Grauer	Dave Garroway
Don Russell	Peter Roberts	Johnny Andrews	Morgan Beatty		Frank Gallop	Don Russell
			1959			
Frank Blair	Hugh Downs	Walter Kiernan	Monty Hall		Ben Grauer	Dave Garroway
Don Russell	Peter Roberts	Johnny Andrews	Morgan Beatty		Frank Gallop	Don Russell
			1960			
Gordon Fraser	?	Walter Kiernan	Monty Hall		Ben Grauer	Dave Garroway
Peter Roberts		Johnny Andrews	Morgan Beatty		Frank Gallop	Peter Roberts

In 1961, *Monitor's* broadcast schedule was reduced to 16 live hours a weekend. The "co-communicators" idea for each segment was dropped, and only one host handled each segment. Some of the hosts below are listed in more than one time slot because their schedules changed during the course of the specific year. If more than one host is listed for a particular segment each year, it means that each of them hosted that segment individually during part of that year.

SATURDAY				SUNDAY	
9 a.m.-noon	3-6 p.m.	7:30-10:30 p.m.		2-6 p.m.	7-10 p.m.
		1961			
Gene Rayburn	Bert Parks	Wayne Howell		Hall March	Dave Garroway
Mel Allen	Gene Rayburn				Gene Rayburn
					Frank McGee
		1962			
Mel Allen	Gene Rayburn	Jim Lowe		Bill Hayes	Frank McGee
		1963			
Mel Allen	Gene Rayburn	Jim Lowe		James Daly	Frank McGee
David Wayne	Ed McMahon				
		1964			
David Wayne	Ed McMahon	Gene Rayburn		James Daly	Frank McGee
					Frank Blair
		1965			
David Wayne	Ed McMahon	Gene Rayburn		Barry Nelson	Frank Blair
		1966			
Gene Rayburn	Ed McMahon	Henry Morgan		Barry Nelson	Frank Blair
		1967			
Gene Rayburn	Ed McMahon	Ted Steele		Henry Morgan	Brad Crandall
		1968			
Gene Rayburn	Ed McMahon	Ted Steele		Henry Morgan	Brad Crandall
		1969			
Gene Rayburn	Joe Garagiola	Murray the K		Henry Morgan	Jim Lowe

In May 1970, Saturday night *Monitor* began airing from 7 to 10 p.m. ET.

	SATURDAY			SUNDAY
9 a.m.-noon	3-6 p.m.	7-10 p.m.	2-6 p.m.	7-10 p.m.
Gene Rayburn	Joe Garagiola	**1970** Murray the K	Ted Brown	Jim Lowe
Gene Rayburn	Bill Cullen	**1971** Murray the K Cindy Adams	Ted Brown	Jim Lowe
Gene Rayburn	Bill Cullen	**1972** Cindy Adams	Ted Brown Art Fleming	Jim Lowe
Gene Rayburn	Bill Cullen	**1973** Don Imus Wolfman Jack Robert W. Morgan	Dan Daniel	Jim Lowe

In 1974, *Monitor's* broadcast schedule changed one last time. The program began airing live on Saturdays from 9 a.m. to 3 p.m. ET with same-day repeats airing from 3 to 9 p.m., and live on Sundays from noon to 6 p.m., with same-day repeats airing from 6 to 9 p.m.

	SATURDAY		SUNDAY
9 a.m.-noon	Noon-3 p.m.	Noon-3 p.m.	3-6 p.m.
Big Wilson	Tony Taylor John B. Tucker	**1974** Bruce Bradley Big Wilson	John B. Tucker
John B. Tucker	Big Wilson	**1975** Big Wilson	John B. Tucker

The final *Monitor* broadcasts aired on January 25-26, 1975. The program ended its live run at 5:58:50 P.M. ET on Sunday, Jan. 26, with John Bartholomew Tucker as the final host. The final sounds ever heard on *Monitor* were the NBC chimes.

About the Author

Dennis Hart is a 20-year veteran of radio and television broadcasting. He has been a radio news director, as well as a television assistant news director, executive producer, assignment manager, anchor and reporter. He has worked in Los Angeles, San Francisco, Detroit, Atlanta, Phoenix, Buffalo and Fresno.

Hart has received an Emmy Award, plus awards presented by the Associated Press, United Press International and the San Francisco Bay Area Press Club.

He also has taught in the journalism departments of Iowa State University and California State University, Northridge. He currently teaches mass communication at California State University, Fresno.

Notes

Chapter 1

1. "TV Sets," *New York Times*, May 4, 1952, p. 11.

2. "A.C. Nielsen Company Program Ratings," *Broadcasting-Telecasting*, June 16, 1952, p. 30.

3. "Will TV Push Radio Out?" *Business Week*, December 27, 1952, p. 27.

4. "TV Homes Hit 19.5 Million in 1952," *Broadcasting-Telecasting*, April 13, 1953, p. 32.

5. "Gen. Sarnoff Details Radio-TV 'Evolution,'" *Broadcasting-Telecasting*, May 4, 1953, p.40.

6. "Address by David Sarnoff," *Broadcasting-Telecasting*, September 21, 1953, p. 110.

7. "A.C. Nielsen Company Program Ratings," *Broadcasting-Telecasting*, July 5, 1954, p. 40.

8. "Nielsen Releases First Auto Listening Report," *Broadcasting-Telecasting*, March 21, 1955, p. 32.

9. "Network Rate Cuts," *Broadcasting-Telecasting*, May 12, 1952, p. 23.

10. "TV Networks Pass Radio in Time Sales," *New York Times*, August 1, 1953, p. 18.

11. "Radio Billings, 1935-1970," *Broadcasting Yearbook 1972*, p. 45.

12. "Address by David Sarnoff," *Broadcasting-Telecasting*, September 21, 1953, pp. 109-110.

13. Jack Gould, "Radio and TV: Catching Up," *New York Times*, December 13, 1953, p. 19.

14. "A Major Speech on Major Issues," *Broadcasting-Telecasting*, September 6, 1954, pp. 78-79.

15. NBC had established two radio networks in the 1920's, known as NBC Red and NBC Blue. In the 1940s the U.S. Supreme Court decided, in effect, that NBC must give up one of its networks. NBC Blue was sold and became ABC.

16. "ABC Radio Expands Specialized Programming," *Broadcasting-Telecasting*, June 1, 1953, p. 7.

17. "NBC Radio's Cott Says Overhaul to Bring 'New, Wonderful' Shows, *Broadcasting-Telecasting*, August 17, 1953, p. 88.

18. "16,000 Question," *Time*, June 27, 1955, p. 70.

19. "Radio—A New Era?" *Newsweek*, June 27, 1955, p. 81.

20. *Ibid.*, p. 80.

21. "Weaver Scans the Way Ahead," *Broadcasting-Telecasting*, February 28, 1955, p. 42.

22. "NBC's 'One Big Weekend Show,'" *Variety*, Feb. 23, 1955, p. 31.

23. Steve White, telephone interview, July 21, 1977.

24. Sylvester L. Weaver Jr., personal interview, July 14, 1977.

25. Weaver, closed-circuit message to NBC affiliates, April 1, 1955.

26. *Ibid.*

27. "NBC Show to Run Round the Clock," *New York Times*, April 8, 1955, p. 29.

28. *NBC Monitor,* January 26, 1975.

Chapter 2

1. "The Folly Was Golden," *Newsweek,* June 29, 1959, p. 60.

2. "Dave Garroway to be *Monitor* Communicator," NBC Radio Press Release, April 19, 1955.

3. Robert Metz, *The Today Show* (New York: New American Library, 1977), p. 7.

4. *NBC Monitor*, January 26, 1975.

5. John Dunning, *Tune in Yesterday* (Englewood Cliffs, New Jersey: Prentice-Hall Inc., 1976), pp. 175-177.

6. "Red Barber to Preside Over 4-Hour NBC Radio *Monitor* Session as Communicator," NBC Radio press release, April 27, 1955.

7. Edward J. Bliss, *Now the News* (New York: Columbia University Press, 1991), p. 223.

8. Frank Blair, *Let's Be Frank* (New York: Doubleday and Company, 1979), p. 308.

9. Hugh Downs, telephone interview, September 25, 2001.

10. "Morgan to *Monitor*," *Broadcasting-Telecasting,* May 30, 1955, p. 9.

11. Dunning, *Tune in Yesterday* , pp. 273-375.

12. Tim Brooks and Earle Marsh, *The Complete Directory to Prime-Time Network TV Shows* (New York: Ballentine Books, 1979), p. 459.

13. Dunning, *Tune in Yesterday,* pp. 81-83.

Chapter 3

1. Jim Fleming, NBC Radio closed-circuit announcement to affiliates, April 1, 1955.

2. NBC Radio press release, April 15, 1955.

3. *Ibid.*

4. *Ibid.*

5. Jack Gould, "Radio: *NBC Monitor* Scans All," *New York Times,* June 13, 1955, p. 45.

6. "Radio—A New Era?" *Newsweek,* June 27, 1955, p. 80.

7. "PI Monitors *Monitor,*" *Printers' Ink*, June 17, 1955, p. 96.

8. *Barry Farber Show*, WOR Radio, December 18, 1974.

9. Gene Garnes Jr., E-mail to author, April 2000.

10. "*Monitor* Trademark," *Broadcasting-Telecasting*, June 13, 1955, p. 93.

11. Sylvester L. Weaver Jr., personal interview, July 14, 1977.

12. *NBC Monitor*, June 12, 1955.

13. "Looking at *Monitor,*" *Broadcasting-Telecasting*, September 14, 1955, p. 89.

14. NBC Radio message to affiliates, June 10, 1955.

15. *Ibid.*

16. Terrence O'Flaherty, *San Francisco Chronicle*, June 10, 1955, p. 15.

Chapter 4

1. *New York Times*, June 12, 1955, p. 1.

2. *New York Times*, June 12, 1955, Section 2.

3. "Premiere," *The New York Times*, June 12, 1955, Section 2, p. 9.

4. *New York Times*, June 12, 1955, Section 2, p. 10.

5. Jim Wilson, E-mail to author, August 13, 2001.

6. *NBC Monitor*, June 12, 1955.

7. *Ibid.*

8. Jack Gould, "Radio: *NBC Monitor* Scans All," *New York Times*, June 13, 1955, p. 45.

9. "The Week in Review," *Time*, June 27, 1955, pp. 69-70.

10. "Radio: A New Era?" *Newsweek*, June 27, 1955, p. 82.

11. "P.I. Monitors *Monitor*," *Printers' Ink*, June 17, 1955, pp. 96-97.

12. *"Monitor,"* *Broadcasting-Telecasting*, June 20, 1955, p. 14.

Chapter 5

1. Advertisement, *New York Times*, June 17, 1955, p. 47.

2. "Molotov on *Monitor*," *Broadcasting-Telecasting*, June 27, 1955, p. 105.

3. "On Radio," *New York Times*, June 18, 1955, p. 35.

4. "On Radio," *New York Times*, June 25, 1955, p. 35.

5. "Week's Radio Programs," *New York Times*, June 26, 1955, p. 13X.

6. . Elliot Drake, telephone interview, June 9, 2001.

7. "On Radio," *New York Times*, July 2, 1955, p. 31.

8. "The Fourth," *New York Times*, July 3, 1955, p. 9X.

9. "Week's Radio Programs," *New York Times,* July 3, 1955, p. 10X.

10. "Many Hands Rule Airwaves on *Monitor* Broadcasts," *New York Times,* July 10, 1955, pp. 8-9X.

11. "On Radio," *New York Times*, September 10, 1955, p. 35.

12. "Week's Radio Programs," *New York Times*, September 11, 1955, p. 12X.

13. "On Radio," *New York Times,* Oct. 1, 1955, p. 39; "Week's Radio Programs," *New York Times*, Oct. 2, 1955, p. 14X.

14. Don Kennedy, E-mail to author, September 28, 2001.

15. *Ibid.*

16. "The 'Folly' Was Golden," *Newsweek*, June 29, 1959, p. 60.

17. *NBC Monitor*, January 25, 1975.

18. Drake, telephone interview, May 19, 2001.

19. *NBC Monitor,* June 12, 1955.

20. *Ibid.,* January 26, 1955.

21. *Ibid.*

22. *Ibid.*

23. *Ibid.,* , March 11, 1962.

24. *Ibid.*, March 22, 1964.

25. *Ibid.*, December 15, 1963.

26. Drake, interview on *The Barry Farber Show*, WOR Radio, Dec. 18, 1974.

27. Charles Garment, telephone interview, August 4, 2001.

28. Bob Dreier, E-mail to author, 2000.

29. Gene Garnes Sr., E-mail to author, September 22, 2001.

30. *Ibid.,* September 24, 2001.

31. *Ibid.,* August 19, 2001.

32. Garment, *Ibid.*

33. *NBC Monitor,* January 26, 1975.

34. Garnes, E-mail to author, September 17, 2001.

35. Steve White, telephone interview, July 21, 1977.

36. Giraud Chester, Garnet R. Garrison and Edgar E. Willis, *Television and Radio* (third edition: New York: Appleton-Century Crofts, 1963), p. 80.

37. *NBC Monitor,* January 26, 1975.

38. Sylvester L. Weaver Jr.,personal interview, July 14, 1977.

Chapter 6

1. Robert Maurer, telephone interview, September 7, 2001.

2. Melissa Blanton, telephone interview, October 27, 2001.

3. Charles Garment, telephone interview, August 4, 2001.

4. Bud Drake, telephone interview, June 2, 2001.

5. Garment, *Ibid.*

6. Drake, telephone interview, June 9, 2001.

7. Maurer, *Ibid.*

8. Gene Garnes Sr., E-mail to author, September 17, 2001.

9. Garment, *Ibid.*

10. *Ibid.*

11 Garment, telephone interview, August 11, 2001.

12. Blanton, *Ibid.*

13. Garment, telephone interview, August 4, 2001.

14. Drake, telephone interview, June 9, 2001.

15. Garment, telephone interview, August 4, 2001.

16. Maurer, *Ibid.*

17. Garment, telephone interview, August 4, 2001.

18. *Ibid.*

19. Drake, telephone interview, June 16, 2001.

20. *Ibid.*

21. Garment, telephone interview, August 4, 2001.

22. *Ibid.*

Chapter 7

1. Charles Garment, telephone interview, August 4, 2001.

2. *Ibid.*

3. Bud Drake, telephone interview, May 19, 2001.

4. *NBC Monitor*, January 26, 1975.

5. Monty Hall, E-mail to author, July 25, 2001.

6. *NBC Monitor*, January 26, 1975.

7. *Ibid.,* January 25, 1975.

8. Hugh Downs, telephone interview, September 25, 2001.

9. *Ibid.*

10. *Ibid.*

11. Hall, *Ibid.*

12. Garment, *Ibid.*

13. *Ibid.*

14. Hall, *Ibid.*

15. *NBC Monitor*, January 25, 1975.

16. *Ibid.*

17. Garment, *Ibid.*

18. Drake, *Ibid.*

19. *NBC Monitor*, August 1967.

Ibid., December 6, 1969.

21. Melissa Blanton, telephone interview, October 27, 2001.

22. Drake, telephone interview, June 2, 2001.

23. Garment, *Ibid.*

24. Gene Garnes Sr., E-mail to author, August 15, 2001.

25. *NBC Monitor*, January 25, 1975.

26. *Ibid*

27. *Ibid.*, January 26, 1975.

28. Blanton, *Ibid.*

29. *NBC Monitor*, November 22, 1969.

30. *Ibid.*, November 29, 1969.

31. *Ibid.*

32. *Ibid.*

33. *Ibid.*

34. *Ibid.*

35. *Ibid.*, December 6, 1969.

36. *Ibid.*, December 13, 1969.

37. Drake, telephone interview, May 19, 2001.

38. *NBC Monitor*, November 22, 1969.

39. *Ibid.*, April 30, 1972.

40. *Ibid.*

41. *Ibid.*, Feb. 21, 1971.

42. *Ibid.*, January 26, 1975.

43. Drake, telephone interview, June 2, 2001.

44. Blanton, *Ibid.*

45. Drake, *Ibid.*

46. *NBC Monitor*, February 22, 1969.

47. *Ibid.*, May 16, 1971.

48. *Ibid.*, December 2, 1972.

49. Jim Lowe, telephone interview, September 26, 2001.

50. *Ibid.*

51. *Ibid.*

52. *Ibid*

53. *Ibid.*

54. *Ibid.*

Chapter 8

1. The information and quotes in this chapter, with the exceptions below, are from telephone interviews with Tedi Thurman on October 7 and 8, 2001.

2. Jack Gould, "Radio: NBC *Monitor* Scans All," *New York Times,* June 13, 1955, p. 45.

3. Promotional trailer, *10,000 Bedrooms*, MGM, 1957.

4. Promotional record, NBC Radio, 1959.

5. Linda Thurman, E-mail to author, October 21, 2001.

6. Thurman, E-mail to author, October 22, 2001.

Chapter 9

1. Ray Goulding, interviewed on *The Barry Farber Show*, WOR Radio, Dec. 18, 1974.

2. *NBC Monitor*, January 26, 1975.

3. *Ibid.*

4. *Ibid.,* January 25, 1975.

5. Hugh Downs, telephone interview, September 25, 2001.

6. Bud Drake, telephone interview, June 16, 2001.

7. *NBC Monitor*, January 25, 1975.

8. *Ibid.*, January 26, 1975.

9. Drake, telephone interview, June 9, 2001.

10. *Ibid.*, June 16, 2001.

11. *NBC Monitor*, January 26, 1975.

12. *Ibid.*

13. Jim Lowe, telephone interview, September 26, 2001.

14. *NBC Monitor, Ibid.*

Chapter 10

1. Pat Weaver, closed-circuit announcement to NBC affiliates, April 1, 1955.

2. "NBC Begins Major Revision in Radio Selling, Schedules," *Broadcasting -Telecasting*, April 4, 1955, pp. 27-28.

3. "*Monitor* Problems," *Broadcasting-Telecasting*, April 4, 1955, p. 5.

4. Gary Dibble, letter to author, October 12, 2001

5. "*Monitor* Progress Told to NBC Radio Affiliates, " *Broadcasting-Telecasting*, May 9, 1955, p. 89.

6. "*Monitor* at Three-Quarter Million Mark," *Broadcasting-Telecasting*, May 16, 1955, p. 129.

7. "*Monitor* Is Launched 70 Percent Network-Sponsored," *Broadcasting-Telecasting*, June 13, 1955, p. 93.

8. Advertisement, *The New York Times*, June 13, 1955, p. 34.

9. "*Monitor* Buyers Cannot Justify Program Purchases, SRA Blasts," *Broadcasting-Telecasting*, June 20, 1955, pp. 90-91.

10. "Radio Networks' Business Shows Signs of Firming Up," *Broadcasting-Telecasting*, July 18, 1955, p. 31.

11. "Network Radio Continues To Improve With Added Sales, More Techniques," *Broadcasting-Telecasting*, July 25, 1955, p. 80.

12. "Quarter-Billion Gross Chalked Up By Radio-TV Networks in Six Months," *Broadcasting-Telecasting*, August 8, 1955, p. 89.

13. "New *Monitor* Business," *Broadcasting-Telecasting*, August 15, 1955, p. 5.

14. "NBC Radio Affiliates Call Meeting; The Puzzler: Shall *Monitor* Expand?" *Broadcasting-Telecasting*, August 22, 1955, p. 76.

15. "NBC Expansion of *Monitor* Evokes Blast from Representatives' Group," *Broadcasting-Telecasting*, September 5, 1955, pp. 94-95.

16. *Ibid.*

17. "Reaction to *Monitor* Extension by NBC Radio Found 'Very Mixed,'" *Broadcasting-Telecasting*, September 12, 1955, p. 7.

18. "CBS Radio Ahead of NBC Radio—Karol," *Broadcasting-Telecasting*, September 1955, pp. 44-45.

19. "Looking at *Monitor*," *Broadcasting-Telecasting*, September 19, 1955, p. 89.

20. *Ibid.*, p. 90.

21. Advertisement, *Broadcasting-Telecasting*, September 19, 1955, pp. 68-69.

22. "*Monitor* Billings Get Hefty Boost," *Broadcasting-Telecasting*, September 26, 1955, p. 92.

23. "NBC Radio Chalks Up $5 Million in 10 Days," *Broadcasting-Telecasting*, March 12, 1956, p. 84.

24. "NBC Yearend Figures Show *Monitor* Take $4 Million Plus," *Broadcasting-Telecasting*, June 11, 1956, p. 90.

25. "NBC Radio Will Top Rivals in Weekend Business—Ayres," *Broadcasting-Telecasting*, July 2, 1956, p. 74.

26. "The 'Folly' Was Golden," *Newsweek*, June 29, 1959, p. 60.

27. "NBC Radio Runs Out of Red Ink," *Broadcasting*, June 20, 1960, pp. 56, 58.

28. "Snowman, Beware," *Newsweek*, June 27, 1960, pp. 98-99.

Chapter 11

1. "Audience on Wheels," *Broadcasting-Telecasting*, September 19, 1955, p. 116.

2. "Traffic Jam," *Broadcasting-Telecasting*," September 19, 1955, p. 118.

3. "Nielsen Ratings," *Broadcasting-Telecasting*, August 1, 1955, p. 36.

4. "Nielsen Ratings," *Broadcasting-Telecasting*, August 29, 1955, p. 36.

5. Advertisement, *Printers' Ink*, August 19, 1955, pp. 46-47.

6. *Ibid.*

7. "Looking at *Monitor*," *Broadcasting-Telecasting*, September 19, 1955, p. 90.

8. "New Look for ABC," *Broadcasting-Telecasting*, September 19, 1955, p. 90.

9. "ABC Sees Chance to Catch Rival TV Networks By 1958," *Broadcasting-Telecasting*, March 5, 1956, p. 70.

10. "All You Need's a Beeper Phone," *Broadcasting-Telecasting*, October 3, 1955, p. 44

11. *Ibid.*

12. *Ibid.*

13. *Ibid.*

14. *Ibid.*

15. *Ibid.*

16. W.T. Koltek, E-mail to author, March 2001.

17. Patrick D. Hazard, "Weaver's Magazine Concept: Notes on Auditioning Radio's New Sound," *The Quarterly of Film, Radio and Television*, June 1956, pp. 419-420.

18. Sydney W. Head, *Broadcasting in America* (Boston: Houghton Mifflin Company, 1956) pp. 224-225.

19. "Cutaway (Goo Goo on Disc)," *Harper's*, April 1956, pp. 78-79.

20. Howard S. Becker, "Radio," *New Republic*, Nov. 28, 1955, p. 21.

21. William Saroyan, "Radio Forever," *American Mercury*, December 1955, pp. 26-27.

22. "*Tonight!*" *Broadcasting-Telecasting*, February 4, 1957, p. 14.

23. "Snowman, Beware," *Newsweek*, June 27, 1960, p. 99.

24. NBC Radio, *Monitor* promotional tape, 1964.

25. NBC Radio, *Monitor* promotional material, 1967.

26. Thomas Frieling, E-mail to author, August 3, 2001.

27. Earl Jones, E-mail to author, July 24, 2001.

28. Douglas Drown, E-mail to author, December 4, 2000.

29. Ralph Gould, E-mail to author, December 30, 2000.

Chapter 12

1. "NBC Radio Affiliates Call Meeting; The Puzzler: Shall *Monitor* Expand?" *Broadcasting-Telecasting,* August 22, 1955, p. 76.

2. Robert Wogan, telephone interview, July 12, 1977.

3. "NBC Radio Raises Compensation Rate," *Broadcasting-Telecasting,* Nov., 19, 1956, pp. 95-96.

4. "On Radio," *New York Times,* January 18, 1957, p. 45.

5. "How and Why NBC Has Charted Its Radio-TV Course," *Broadcasting -Telecasting,* September 9, 1957, p. 126.

6. Val Adams, "Radio 'Comeback' Seen By Sarnoff," *New York Times,* March 31, 1958, p. 45.

7. "Radio Network Showsheet," *Broadcasting,* July 6, 1959, pp. 93-95.

8. "The 'Folly' Was Golden," *Newsweek,* June 29, 1959, p. 60.

9. "NBC Radio Shows Its 'Bikini,'" *Broadcasting,* November 16, 1959, p. 72.

10. "NBC Radio's *Monitor* Gets Spring Revamp," *Broadcasting,* March 6, 1961, p. 84.

11. *Ibid.*

12. Wogan, *Ibid.*

13. "Radio Never Lost Audience," *Broadcasting,* December 11, 1961, p. 64.

14. Wogan, *Ibid.*

15. *Ibid.*

16. Charles Garment, telephone interview, August 4, 2001.

17. *Ibid.*

18. Sam J. Slate and Joe Cook, *It Sounds Impossible* (New York: The Macmillan Company, 1963), pp. 222-223.

19. Sylvester L. Weaver Jr., personal interview, July 14, 1977.

20. Speech by Robert Wogan at the NBC Radio Affiliate Executive Committee Meeting, New York, October 6, 1970.

21. *Ibid.*

22. *Ibid.*

23. Wogan, telephone interview, July 12, 1977.

24. Steve White, telephone interview, July 21, 1977.

25. Bud Drake, telephone interview, July 21, 1977.

26. NBC Radio promotional brochure, 1971.

27. Wogan, *Ibid.*

Chapter 13

1. *NBC Monitor*, November 10, 1973.

2. *Ibid.*

3. NBC promotion, 1973.

4. Robert Wogan, telephone interview, July 12, 1977.

5. NBC Radio report to affiliated stations, June 12, 1973.

6. NBC management bulletin, October 22, 1973.

7. Wogan, letter to author, October 30, 1973.

8. "Bell Tolls for Chimes as NBC Trademark," *New York Times*, November 1, 1973, p. 25.

9. "Station Manager's Bulletin," NBC Radio, December 14, 1973.

10. Steve White, telephone interview, July 21, 1977.

11. Bud Drake, telephone interview, July 21, 1977.

12. NBC Radio program information, April 3, 1974.

Chapter 14

1. *New York Times,* January 26, 1975, p. 1.

2. "Program Information," NBC Radio memo to affiliates, February 5, 1974.

3. "Program Info," NBC Radio memo to affiliates, March 6, 1974.

4. "Program Info," NBC Radio memo to affiliates, March 27, 1974.

5. "Program Info," NBC Radio memo to affiliates, April 3, 1974.

6. "*Monitor's* Finally Made It 'Big,'" NBC Radio memo to affiliates, 1974.

7. Bud Drake, telephone interview, June 16, 2001.

8. "Station Manager FYI," NBC Radio memo to affiliates, July 15, 1974.

9. *Ibid.*

10. "No. 2 Network for NBC Radio To Be All-News," *Broadcasting,* February 10, 1975, p. 80.

11. "NBC Tries All-News Radio," *Business Week,* June 20, 1975, p. 86.

12. Charles Garment, telephone interview, August 4, 2001.

13. *Ibid.*

14. "Station Manager FYI," NBC Radio memo to affiliates, December 5, 1974.

15. "*Monitor* to End on NBC Radio; Restyled Network Service Set," *New York Times*, December 5, 1974, p. 94.

16. "A Network Landmark Doomed to be Razed," *Broadcasting*, December 9, 1974, p. 59.

17. Robert Wogan, telephone interview, July 12, 1977.

18. Steve White, telephone interview, July 21, 1977

19. Sylvester L. Weaver Jr., personal interview, July 14, 1977.

20. *Ibid.*

21. Barry Farber, WOR Radio, December 18, 1974.

22. "*NBC Monitor* Commercial Schedule Advance for December 21-22, 1974," NBC Radio memo to affiliates, Dec. 6, 1974.

23. "*NBC Monitor* Commercial Schedule Advance for December 28-29, 1974," NBC Radio memo to affiliates, December 13, 1974.

24. "NBC *Monitor* Commercial Schedule Advance for January 4-5, 1975," NBC Radio memo to affiliates, December 20, 1974.

25. Garment, *Ibid.*

26. *NBC Monitor*, January 26, 1975.

27. *Ibid.*

28. *Ibid.*

29. *Ibid.*

30 *Ibid.*

31. *Ibid.*

32. *Ibid.*

33. *Ibid.*

34. *Ibid.*

35. *Ibid.*

36. *Ibid.*

37. *Ibid.*

38. *Ibid.*

39. *Ibid.*

Epilogue

1. Associated Press, January 27, 1975.

2. Sylvester L. Weaver Jr., letter to author, January 22, 1979.

3. Bob Maurer, telephone interview, September 7, 2001.

4. Bud Drake, telephone interview, July 7, 2001.

5. Charles Garment, telephone interview, August 4, 2001.

0-595-21395-2

CPSIA information can be obtained at www.ICGtesting.com
Printed in the USA
LVOW040737230912

299908LV00002B/76/A